TESTIMONIES ON
SEXUAL BEHAVIOR,
ADULTERY,
AND DIVORCE

A compilation from the writings of

ELLEN G. WHITE

TESTIMONIES ON SEXUAL BEHAVIOR, ADULTERY, AND DIVORCE

A compilation from the writings of

ELLEN G. WHITE

THE ELLEN G. WHITE ESTATE
12501 Old Columbia Pike
Silver Spring, Maryland 20904

Library of Congress Catalog Number: 89-61341

ISBN 0-8163-0853-5

PREFACE

This book is not intended for general circulation. It has been prepared especially for the benefit of church administrators and other ministers who must deal with questionable or immoral conduct.

Many of the letters in this volume were addressed to errant ministerial laborers. Since Ellen White corresponded largely with ministers and other gospel workers, this should come as no surprise. However, in spite of the faults and sins of those to whom she wrote, Ellen White had great confidence in the ministry of the Seventh-day Adventist Church. At the age of 85 she sent two messages to be read to the General Conference session of 1913. In the first message she assured the delegates,

> "While I still feel the deepest anxiety over the attitude that some are taking toward important measures connected with the development of the cause of God in the earth, yet I have strong faith in the workers throughout the field, and believe that as they meet together and humble themselves before the Lord and consecrate themselves anew to His service, they will be enabled to do His will."—2SM 401, 402.

In her second and final message to the conference Ellen White declared:

> "When in the night season I am unable to sleep, I lift my heart in prayer to God, and He strengthens me

and gives me the assurance that He is with His ministering servants in the home field and in distant lands. I am encouraged and blessed as I realize that the God of Israel is still guiding His people, and that He will continue to be with them, even to the end.''—2SM 406.

These expressions of confidence make clear that the moral problems dealt with in the letters quoted in this volume were not general or widespread. Nevertheless, since contemporary moral problems are similar to those of past decades, we believe that many letters written by Ellen White a century ago contain warnings and appeals that need to be heard today. Concerning the use of her letters, Ellen White said:

"I am endeavoring by the help of God to write letters that will be a help, not merely to those to whom they are addressed, but to many others who need them.''—Letter 79, 1905.

The present compilation is not designed to serve as a manual of rules for dealing with immorality, infidelity, or unscriptural divorce and remarriage. No manual could cover every possible moral irregularity. When W. C. White was asked for an authoritative statement from his mother that would serve as a standard by which to settle all cases of unscriptural marriage, he replied:

"After reading the documents I sent you today, you will say, Well, he has not given me anything authoritative from Sister White that directly answers the question. But I think you will see from what I am sending you that it was Sister White's intention that there should not go forth from her pen anything that could be used as a law or a rule dealing with these questions of marriage, divorce, remarriage, and adultery. She felt that the different cases where the devil had led men into serious entanglements were so varied and so serious, that should she write anything that could be considered as a rule for settling such cases, it would be misunderstood and misused."— W. C. White to C. P. Bollman, Jan. 6, 1931.

We concur fully with Ellen White's view. Moral problems are complex. No two situations are exactly alike. Each will require careful study; and although the differences may be minor, each situation will require its own solution. The Holy Spirit will always be needed as a divine Guide and Counselor to help those who are grappling with moral problems.

All given names in this book are genuine, but, in the various problem cases cited, letters of the alphabet have been substituted for the surnames. All chapter titles and sub-headings have been supplied.

It is our hope and prayer that in the hands of an ever-learning and truly caring church, the materials in this compilation will contribute to the elevation of moral standards in the church, and at the same time provide comfort, encouragement, and hope for those whose complex moral problems seem beyond human solution.

The Trustees of the
Ellen G. White Estate

CONTENTS

Section VII—Counsels to People With Moral Problems

Section VIII—Unscriptural Marriages

Section IX—Counsels to Church Administrators

Section X—Love for the Erring and Tempted

ABBREVIATIONS

AH	*The Adventist Home*
AM	*Appeal to Mothers*
4BC	*The Seventh-day Adventist Bible Commentary,* vol. 4
DA	*The Desire of Ages*
CG	*Child Guidance*
Ed	*Education*
FE	*Fundamentals of Christian Education*
GCB	*General Conference Bulletin*
Letter	Ellen G. White Letter
LYL	*Letters to Young Lovers*
1MCP	*Mind, Character, and Personality,* vol. 1
MB	*Thoughts From the Mount of Blessing*
MH	*The Ministry of Healing*
Ms	Ellen G. White Manuscript
PP	*Patriarchs and Prophets*
RH	*Review and Herald*
4SGa	*Spiritual Gifts,* vol. 4a
1SM	*Selected Messages,* book 1 (2SM and 3SM for books 2 and 3)
SpT Series B	*Special Testimonies,* Series B
ST	*Signs of the Times*
1T	*Testimonies for the Church* (2T, etc., for vols. 2-9)
TM	*Testimonies to Ministers*

Section I

MARRIAGE

1. Important Facts And Principles

God's Original Design. God celebrated the first marriage. Thus the institution has for its originator the Creator of the universe. "Marriage is honorable"; it was one of the first gifts of God to man, and it is one of the two institutions that, after the fall, Adam brought with him beyond the gates of Paradise. When the divine principles are recognized and obeyed in this relation, marriage is a blessing; it guards the purity and happiness of the race, it provides for man's social needs, it elevates the physical, the intellectual, and the moral nature.—PP 46.

Approved by God Today. *There is in itself no sin in eating and drinking, or in marrying and giving in marriage. It was lawful to marry in the time of Noah, and it is lawful to marry now, if that which is lawful is properly treated, and not carried to sinful excess.—RH Sept. 25, 1888.

---

*In 1885 Ellen White stated, "In this age of the world, as the scenes of earth's history are soon to close and we are about to enter upon the time of trouble such as never was, the fewer the marriages contracted, the better for all, both men and women."— 5T 366. Obviously, she believed that the end of the world was imminent. But Christ's return has been delayed. In 1901 Ellen White wrote, "We may have to remain here in this world because of insubordination many more years." She continued giving counsel on marital relationships throughout her lifetime.

In regard to marriage, I would say, Read the Word of God. Even in this time, the last days of this world's history, marriages take place among Seventh-day Adventists. . . .

We have, as a people, never forbidden marriage, except in cases where there were obvious reasons that marriage would be misery to both parties. And even then, we have only advised and counseled.—Letter 60, 1900.

A Preparation for Heaven. Let them remember that the home on earth is to be a symbol of and a preparation for the home in heaven.—MH 363.

God wants the home to be the happiest place on earth, the very symbol of the home in heaven. Bearing the marriage responsibilities in the home, linking their interests with Jesus Christ, leaning upon His arm and His assurance, husband and wife may share a happiness in this union that angels of God commend.—AH 102.

A Lifelong Union. Marriage, a union for life, is a symbol of the union between Christ and His church.—7T 46.

In the youthful mind marriage is clothed with romance, and it is difficult to divest it of this feature, with which imagination covers it, and to impress the mind with a sense of the weighty responsibilities involved in the marriage vow. This vow links the destinies of the two individuals with bonds which naught but the hand of death should sever.

Every marriage engagement should be carefully considered, for marriage is a step taken for life. Both the man and the woman should carefully consider whether they can cleave to each other through the vicissitudes of life as long as they both shall live.—AH 340.

From an Elevated Standpoint. Those professing to be Christians should not enter the marriage relation until the matter has been carefully and prayerfully considered from an elevated standpoint, to see if God can be glorified by the union. Then they should duly consider the result of every privilege of the marriage relation, and sanctified principle should be the basis of every action.—RH Sept. 19, 1899.

Examine carefully to see if your married life would be happy or inharmonious and wretched. Let the questions be raised, Will this union help me heavenward? Will it increase my love for God? And will it enlarge my sphere of usefulness in this life? If these reflections present no drawback, then in the fear of God move forward.—FE 104, 105.

All in the Name of the Lord Jesus. One about to marry a wife should stop to consider candidly why he takes this step. Is his wife to be his helper, his companion, his equal, or will he pursue toward her such a course that she cannot have an eye single to the glory of God? Will he venture to give loose rein to his passions and see how much care and taxation he can subject his wife to without extinguishing life, or will he study the meaning of the words, "Whatsoever ye do, in word or deed, do all in the name of the Lord Jesus"?—Ms 152, 1899.

The Necessity of Careful Preparation. Before assuming the responsibilities involved in marriage, young men and young women should have such an experience in practical life as will prepare them for its duties and its burdens. Early marriages are not to be encouraged. A relation so important as marriage and so far-reaching in its results should not be entered upon hastily, without sufficient preparation, and before the mental and physical powers are well developed.—MH 358.

My dear Emma,* there is not a person I could take to my heart as heartily as yourself. Yet I advise you . . . to . . . move cautiously, weigh every move. You are making a move which will be lasting. Therefore do not move hastily. Do not get entirely swallowed up in this one matter, marriage.—Letter 7, 1869.

Consultation With God. The words of Christ should ever be borne in mind: "As it was in the days of Noah, so shall it be also in the days of the Son of man." They married wives, they were given in marriage until the day that Noah entered into the ark, and the flood came and destroyed them all. We see the same infatuation in regard to marriage. Youth, and even men and women, who ought to be wise and discerning, act as if bewitched upon this question. Satanic power seems to take possession of them. Courtship and marriage is the all-absorbing theme. The most indiscreet marriages are formed. God is not consulted. Human feelings, desires, and passions bear down everything before them, until the die is cast. Untold misery is the result of this state of things, and God is dishonored. The marriage bed is not sanctified or holy. Shall there not be a decided change in reference to this important matter?—Letter 84, 1888.

---

*Written June 17, 1869, to Emma McDearmon, who was 21 when she married Ellen White's son, Edson, on his 21st birthday, July 28, 1870. Emma was born on November 16, 1848. Ellen White's other son, William C. White, was 21 when he married Mary Kelsey, who was not quite 19.

With Believers Only. The wife of Lot was a selfish, ir-religious woman, and her influence was exerted to separate her husband from Abraham. But for her, Lot would not have remained in Sodom, deprived of the counsel of the wise, God-fearing patriarch. The influence of his wife and the associations of that wicked city would have led him to apostatize from God had it not been for the faithful instruction he had early received from Abraham. The marriage of Lot and his choice of Sodom for a home were the first links in a chain of events fraught with evil to the world for many generations.

No one who fears God can without danger connect himself with one who fears Him not. "Can two walk together, except they be agreed?" (Amos 3:3). The happiness and prosperity of the marriage relation depend upon the unity of the parties; but between the believer and the unbeliever there is a radical difference of tastes, inclinations, and purposes. They are serving two masters, between whom there can be no concord. However pure and correct one's principles may be, the influence of an unbelieving companion will have a tendency to lead away from God. . . . The marriage of Christians with the ungodly is forbidden in the Bible. The Lord's direction is, "Be ye not unequally yoked together with un-believers."2 Corinthians 6:14, 17, 18. —PP 174, 175.

Let not unholy bonds be formed between the children of God and the friends of the world. Let there not be marriages made between believers and unbelievers. Let the people of God take their stand firmly for truth and righteousness.— RH July 31, 1894.

Great care should be taken by Christian youth in the formation of friendships and in the choice of companions. Take heed, lest what you now think to be pure gold turns out to be base metal. Worldly associations tend to place obstructions in the way of your service to God, and many souls are ruined by unhappy unions, either business or matrimonial, with those who can never elevate or ennoble. Never should God's people venture upon forbidden ground. Marriage between believers and unbelievers is forbidden by God. But too often the unconverted heart follows its own desires, and marriages unsanctioned by God are formed. Because of this, many men and women are without hope and without God in the world. Their noble aspirations are dead; by a chain of circumstances they are held in Satan's net.—RH Feb. 1, 1906.

God's Claims First. Though the companion of your choice were in all other respects worthy (which he is not), yet he has not accepted the truth for this time; he is an unbeliever, and you are forbidden of heaven to unite yourself with him. You cannot, without peril to your soul, disregard this divine injunction. . . . To connect with an unbeliever is to place yourself on Satan's ground. You grieve the Spirit of God and forfeit His protection. Can you afford to have such terrible odds against you in fighting the battle for everlasting life?

You may say: "But I have given my promise, and shall I now retract it?" I answer: If you have made a promise contrary to the Scriptures, by all means retract it without delay, and in humility before God repent of the infatuation that led you to make so rash a pledge. Far better take back such a promise, in the fear of God, than keep it and thereby dishonor your Maker.—5T 364, 365.

The Lord has in His Word plainly instructed His people not to unite themselves with those who have not His love and fear before them. Such companions will seldom be satisfied with the love and respect which are justly theirs. They will constantly seek to gain from the God-fearing wife or husband some favor which shall involve a disregard of the divine requirements. To a godly man, and to the church with which he is connected, a worldly wife or a worldly friend is as a spy in the camp, who will watch every opportunity to betray the servant of Christ, and expose him to the enemy's attacks.

Satan is constantly seeking to strengthen his power over the people of God by inducing them to enter into alliance with the hosts of darkness.—ST Oct. 6, 1881.

2. Cautions and Counsels

A Child Bride.* Poor girl! She married when but a mere child, needing her mother's care. It was an unhappy event. She was a young child. Her health was poor and her husband was severe and arbitrary. This child was too young for a companion. He could not respect her as such. She was but a child. He ruled her like a tyrant. Already they are parted, she hating him most thoroughly and he without love for her.—Ms 4, 1873.

Long Engagements Not Wise. I am sorry that you have entangled yourself in any courtship with Nellie A. In the first place, your anxiety upon this question is premature. Sound judgment and discretion will bid you wait for one or two years. But for you to select one to be in your mind and affections that length of time would not be prudent for you or just to the one to whom you pay your address.

Premature Affections. I speak what I know in this matter,

---

*The age of this girl at the time of her marriage is not known.

that the very best course for you and for Nellie is to give this matter up entirely, for no good can come of it. In continuing your attentions to her, you will be unfitting yourself for your office duties and placing obstructions in your way for a thorough education and for the habits of body and mind to become settled. Even to bind your affections prematurely is doing yourself and any young lady injustice. . . .

I have been shown the evil of these early attachments, especially when a young man is away from the home roof and must select his companion without the discriminating eye of his mother. It is not safe for you to trust to your own judgment. Early anxiety upon the subject of courtship and marriage will divert your mind from your work and studies, and will produce in you and the one whom you flatter with your attentions a demoralizing influence. There will be in you both a vain forwardness in manners, and infatuation will seize you both, and you will be so completely blinded in regard to your influence and example that you will, if you continue in the course you have entered upon, expose yourselves to criticism and demand that censure should be passed upon your course.

This courtship and marriage is the most difficult to manage, because the mind becomes so bewildered and enchanted that duty to God and everything else becomes tame and uninteresting, and calm and mature thought is the last thing to be exercised in this matter of the gravest importance. Dear youth, I speak to you as one who knows. Wait till you have some just knowledge of yourself and of the world, of the bearing and character of young women, before you let the subject of marriage possess your thoughts.

After the Honeymoon. I could cite you many who are now mourning over their extreme folly and madness in their marriage, when mourning will avail them nothing. They find themselves exposed to temptations they never dreamed of; they find traits of character in the object of their choice above which they cannot elevate them, and therefore they accept the inevitable and come to their level. Nellie A will never elevate you. She has not in her the hidden powers which, developed, would make a woman of judgment and ability to stand by your side, to help you in the battles of life. She lacks force of character. She has not depth of thought and compass of mind that will be a help to you. You see the surface and it is all there is. In a little while, should you marry, the charm would be broken. The novelty of the married life having ceased, you will see things in their real light, and find out you have made a sad mistake.

Need of Mature Judgment. Maturity of judgment will give you much better discernment and power of discrimination to know the truth. Your character needs forming, your judgment needs strength before you entertain the thought of marriage. You are not now prepared to judge of another, and do not be betrayed into committing a grievous indiscretion, if not crime, for which the bitter regrets and tears of afterlife will bring no relief. The child, the mere undisciplined immature schoolgirl, the Miss, dependent upon the discretion of parents and guardians, has no reason to listen to anything like courtship or marriage. She should decline all special attentions which would have the least likelihood to lead to any such results, and devote herself intently to making herself as perfect a woman as possible, that her life may be useful, and learn a trade that she will have employment and be independent.

Intellectual Basis of True Love. Love is a sentiment so sacred that but few know what it is. It is a term used but not understood. The warm glow of impulse, the fascination of one young person for another, is not love; it does not deserve the name. True love has an intellectual basis, a deep, thorough knowledge of the object loved. But this catching up with objects and bestowing on them the thoughts and affections, is without reason, without judgment, and is excessive, temporary, and sensual.

Remember that impulsive love is perfectly blind. It will as soon be placed on unworthy objects as worthy. Command such love to stand still and cool. Give place to genuine thought and deep, earnest reflection. Is this object of your affection, in the scale of intelligence and moral excellence, in deportment and cultivated manners, such that you will feel a pride in presenting her to your father's family, to acknowledge her in all society as the object of your choice, one whose society, conversational powers, and manners will interest and satisfy your most grand expectations? Will Nellie fill this bill? I answer decidedly, No, she will not.

Importance of Family Backgrounds. Let time teach you discretion, and what the genuine claims of love are, before it is allowed to step one inch further. Ruin, fearful ruin, is before you in this life and the next, if you pursue the course you have been following. Look to the family history. Two families are to be brought into close and sacred connection. Perfection in all these relations is not, of course, to be expected, but you would make a most cruel move to marry a girl whose ancestry and relatives would degrade and mortify you, or tempt you to slight and ignore them.

Counsel From Parents and Close Friends. It is safe to make haste slowly in these matters. Give yourself sufficient time for observation on every point, and then do not trust to your own judgment, but let the mother who loves you, and your father, and confidential friends, make critical observation of the one you feel inclined to favor. Trust not to your own judgment, and marry no one whom you feel will not be an honor to your father and mother, [but] one who has intelligence and moral worth. The girl who gives over her affections to a man, and invites his attention by her advances, hanging around where she will be noticed of him unless he shall appear rude, is not the girl you want to associate with. Her conversation is cheap and frequently without depth.

No Marriage Preferable to a Mismatch. Nellie A will not be as much prepared by cultivated manners and useful knowledge to marry at twenty-five as some girls would be at eighteen. But men generally of your age have a very limited knowledge of character, and no just idea of how foolish a man can make himself by fancying a young girl who is not fit for him in any sense. It will be far better not to marry at all than to be unfortunately married, but seek counsel of God in all these things. Be so calm, so submissive to the will of God, that you will not be in a fever of excitement and unqualified for His service by your attachments.—Letter 59, 1880.

Need of Similar Temperaments. I learned that you thought of marrying a sister named Anna Hale. This aroused me to hasten out the things which I had seen. Your organization is not of that refined order that you can make a woman of her fine, sensitive nature happy. It is not at all in God's order that such temperaments as hers and yours should unite. You possess a large proportion of the animal. You have strong animal passions which have not been controlled as they should have been. The more noble, elevated powers of the mind have been servant to the lower, or baser, passions. You have failed to be sanctified through the truth which you profess, have failed to be a partaker of the divine nature, having escaped the corruption that is in the world through lust.

Anna Hale is not a person who can endure the roughs of life. She is a frail flower and would soon droop and die if exposed to storm and neglect. You have not in your previous marriage understood the wants of a woman. You have not appreciated her delicate organism. You failed, greatly failed, with your first wife. She possessed a powerful constitution which can scarcely be equaled for power of endurance, but she presumed too much. Your anxiety to acquire led you both to overtax yourselves and be swallowed up in the cares of this life, and to neglect present happiness and comfort, looking ahead to a time when you should have more of this world's goods, and then you could afford to look after the comforts of life.

You have made a sad mistake. The life of your wife was sacrificed. She might have lived. She ought to have lived. But you knew so little of woman's organism that you failed to have care, and neglected the preparation you should have made for her comfort. To a very great degree you possess the temperament of your father.

When you seek a wife, go not among the delicate and refined, where the intellectual predominates. Select you a wife among that class more in accordance with your organization. You cannot make a person of refined spiritual temperament happy.—Letter 21, 1868.

Faithfulness in the Parental Home. It is by faithfulness to duty in the parental home that the young are to prepare themselves for homes of their own. Let them here practice self-denial and manifest kindness, courtesy, and Christian sympathy. Thus love will be kept warm in the heart, and he who goes out from such a household to stand at the head of a family of his own will know how to promote the happiness of her whom he has chosen as a companion for life.

Marriage, instead of being the end of love, will be only its beginning.—PP 176.

I beg of you, yes, I warn you in the name of my Master, do not enter the marriage relation and take upon yourself the responsibilities and obligation of the marriage vows until you are changed in heart and life. When you can make your own home happy, be a blessing to your father and mother, your brothers and sister, then you can understand the duties involved in the marriage relation.—Ms 2, 1871.

3. Individuality

Individuality of the Wife. A woman that will submit to be ever dictated to in the smallest matters of domestic life, who will yield up her identity, will never be of much use or blessing in the world, and will not answer the purpose of God in her existence. She is a mere machine to be guided by another's will and another's mind. God has given each one, men and women, an identity, an individuality, that they must act in the fear of God for themselves.—Letter 25, 1885.

Separate Identity of Husband and Wife. I was shown that although a couple were married, gave themselves to each other by a most solemn vow in the sight of heaven and holy angels, and the two were one, yet each had a separate identity which the marriage covenant could not destroy. Although bound to one another, yet each has an influence to exert in the world, and they should not be so selfishly engrossed with each other as to shut themselves away from society and bury their usefulness and influence.—Letter 9, 1864.

A Passive Wife. Let the wife decide that it is the husband's prerogative to have full control of her body, and to mold her mind to suit his in every respect, to run in the same channel as his own, and she yields her individuality; her identity is lost, merged in that of her husband. She is a mere machine for his will to move and control, a creature of his pleasure. He thinks for her, decides for her, and acts for her. She dishonors God in occupying this passive position. She has a responsibility before God, which it is her duty to preserve.

When the wife yields her body and mind to the control of her husband, being passive to his will in all things, sacrificing her conscience, her dignity, and even her identity, she loses the opportunity of exerting that mighty influence for good which she should possess, to elevate her husband.—RH Sept. 26, 1899.

Love for Christ, Love for Each Other. Neither the husband nor the wife should merge his or her individuality in that of the other. Each has a personal relation to God. Of Him each is to ask, "What is right?" "What is wrong?" "How may I best fulfill life's purpose?" Let the wealth of your affection flow forth to Him who gave His life for you. Make Christ first and last and best in everything. As your love for Him becomes deeper and stronger, your love for each other will be purified and strengthened.

The spirit that Christ manifests toward us is the spirit that husband and wife are to manifest toward each other. "As Christ also hath loved us," "walk in love." "As the church is subject unto Christ, so let the wives be to their own husbands in everything. Husbands, love your wives, even as Christ also loved the church, and gave Himself for it."

No Arbitrary Control. Neither the husband nor the wife should attempt to exercise over the other an arbitrary control. Do not try to compel each other to yield to your wishes. You cannot do this and retain each other's love. Be kind, patient and forbearing, considerate and courteous. By the grace of God you can succeed in making each other happy, as in your marriage vow you promised to do.—RH Dec. 10, 1908.

I was then shown his daughter-in-law. She is beloved of God, but held in servile bondage, fearing, trembling, desponding, doubting, and very nervous. This sister should not feel that she must yield her will to a godless youth who has less years upon his head than herself. She should remember that her marriage does not destroy her individuality. God has claims upon her higher than any earthly claim. Christ has bought her with His own blood. She is not her own. She fails to put her entire trust in God, and submits to yield her convictions, her conscience, to an overbearing, tyrannical man, fired up by Satan whenever his satanic majesty can work effectually through him to intimidate this trembling, shrinking soul. She has so many times been thrown into agitation that her nervous system is shattered, and she is merely a wreck.

Is it the will of the Lord that this sister should be in this state and God be robbed of her service? No. Her marriage was a deception of the devil. Yet now she should make the best of it, treat her husband with tenderness, and make him as happy as she can without violating her conscience; for if he remains in his rebellion, this world is all the heaven he will have. But to deprive herself of the privilege of meetings, to gratify an overbearing husband possessing the spirit of the dragon, is not according to God's will. He wants this trembling soul to flee to Him. He will be a covert to her. He will be like the shadow of a great rock in a weary land.

Only have faith, trust in God and He will strengthen and bless. All three of her children are susceptible to the influences of the truth and Spirit of God. Could these children be as favorably situated as are many Sabbathkeeping children, all would be converted and enlist in the army of the Lord.—2T 99, 100.

The Head of the House. Mary, . . . I wish in all sisterly and motherly kindness to kindly warn you upon another point. I have often noticed before others a manner you have in speaking to John in rather a dictating manner, the tone of your voice sounding impatient. Mary, others notice this and have spoken of it to me. It hurts your influence.

We women must remember that God has placed us subject to the husband. He is the head, and our judgment and views and reasonings must agree with his, if possible. If not, the preference in God's Word is given to the husband where it is not a matter of conscience. We must yield to the head.—Letter 5, 1861.

An Overbearing Husband. I have a few words to say in regard to your marriage, not by revelation but permission. Yes, I feel compelled by the Spirit of the Lord to say to you [that] I have had less confidence in your integrity since your marriage than I have had heretofore. My heart was greatly burdened. I knew you were not qualified to make a proper husband for Sister Drake. If you had permitted her to lay her case before us, we could have advised her according to the light God has given us of your case. You knew this, therefore you were unwilling to have us consulted. Brother R, I believe that your motives in this marriage were purely selfish. I do not believe you had a thought of the good of Sister Drake or the glory of God. You urged yourself upon her without consulting those who knew you best. You hurried this matter off with your own hasty spirit that you have ever possessed.

Stewardship of Means. Your course since your marriage, in taking possession of and controlling the means of her [whom] you had made your wife, shows your motives to be wrong. All these things are against you and show on your part very deep selfishness and a dictatorial spirit which God would not have her submit to. Her marriage does not make null and void her stewardship. It does not destroy her identity. Her individuality should be preserved if she would glorify God with her body and spirit, which are His. Her individuality cannot be submerged in you. She has duties she owes to God which you have no right to interfere with. God has claims upon her which you cannot meet. In the providence of God she has become His steward, and this she should refuse to yield to you or any other one.

You have not wisdom more exact and perfect than hers which should lead her to give to you the stewardship of her means. She has developed a far better character than yourself, and has a better balanced mind than yourself. She can manage this means in her hands more wisely, more judiciously, and more to the glory of God than yourself. You are a man of extremes. You move by impulse and are most of the time more directly under the control of evil angels than the angels of God.—Letter 4, 1870.

Improper Motives. I need not tell you I deeply regret your marriage. You are not the man that can make your wife happy. You love yourself too well to be kind, attentive, patient, affectionate, and sympathizing. How tenderly you should now treat her whom you have married. How carefully you should study to make her not regret that she has united her destiny with yours. God looks upon the course you have pursued in this matter, and you will be without excuse for the course you have taken. God reads your motives. You now have an opportunity to exhibit your true self, to demonstrate whether you were actuated by true love or deep, selfish interest in your marriage. You married, I have no doubt, thinking you would come in possession of property and have the handling of it as you pleased.

Importance of Love and Tenderness. You have no right to dictate to your wife as you would a child. You have not earned a valuable reputation of goodness that would require reverence. You need, considering your failures in the past, to take a humble position and divest yourself of a dignity you have not earned. You are too weak a man to require submission to your will without an appeal. You have a work to do to govern yourself. . . .

You should never set yourself above your wife. She needs kindness and love, which will be reflected back to you again. If you expect her to love you, you must earn this love by manifesting love and tenderness in your words and actions for her. You have in your keeping the happiness of your wife. Your course says to her, In order for you to be happy, you must yield your will up fully to mine; you must submit to do my pleasure. You have taken special delight in exercising your authority because you thought you could do so. But time will show that if you pursue the course your own temperament would lead you to do, you will not inspire in the heart of your wife love, but will wean her affections from you, and she will in the end despise that authority, the power of which she has never felt before in her married life. You are certainly making hard and bitter work for yourself, and you will reap what you are sowing.

A Mother's Responsibility to Her Child. I dare not do

otherwise than speak to you plainly. The case demands it. How is the marriage of Sister Drake to you improving her condition? Not a whit; but your course is making her life a bitterness, her lot almost unbearable. I knew how it would be as soon as I heard of your marriage. She thought she was to have one to help her take care of her boy, but you would tear the mother from her son, and require her to yield her parental care and affection for her son to you who have only your marriage to plead why this should be so. You have done nothing to earn this great sacrifice. You have not pursued a course to even gain her confidence. Yet you demand this great sacrifice, the separation of the mother from her son. You may plead that you understand the case, while we plead [that] you know but little about it. Instead of your feeling it to be your duty to be patient and affectionate, and judiciously manage the case of this her son, you take a course that a heartless, unfeeling tyrant would pursue.

I would advise the mother to move in the fear of God and not allow a comparative stranger to come in, claiming the title of husband, and separate her child from her affection and care. God has not released that mother from her responsibility because she has married you. You do not possess true love. You are not acquainted with the pure article. If you were, you would never have pursued the course you have.—Letter 4, 1870.

4. Remarriage of Widows and Widowers

Prospective Marriage in Old Age. Dear Brother Hare: I will say in regard to your first letter received in the mail before the last, I have no special light upon this subject and cannot give you information upon the point that interests you. I advise you to consult with Wesley Hare and his wife, as they know the one you have in mind and would be the proper counsellors. I know, as you say, that you must be lonely in your old age, and if there is one whom you could love, and who would reciprocate that love, I see no objection. But as I do not know the lady you have in mind, I cannot speak as could one who knows both parties.

One thing is certain: You know that He whom you have served for many years will be to you a safe Counsellor. Rest your case with Him who never makes a mistake. Our time now, both yours and mine, is short, and we need to be ripening for the future immortal life. Christ says, "Let not your heart be troubled: ye believe in God, believe also in Me. In My Father's house are many mansions: if it were not so, I would have told you. I go to prepare a place for you. And if I go and prepare a place for you, I will come again, and receive you unto Myself; that where I am, there ye may be also" [John 14:1-3]. Let us rejoice in this, and take on just as few worries as possible.

The Later Years a Time of Repose. The invitation to old and young is, "Come unto Me, all ye that labor and are heavy laden, and I will give you rest. Take My yoke upon you, and learn of Me; for I am meek and lowly in heart; and ye shall find rest unto your souls" [Matt. 11:28-30]. Thank the Lord, with heart and soul and voice, that there is a haven of rest, sweet rest. It is your privilege, and it is my privilege, to accept the invitation, and rest. We want now that our remnant of life should be as free as possible from every perplexity and care, that we shall have repose in the life of Christ. "My yoke," He says, "is easy, and My burden is light."

The Lord will not disappoint any who put their trust in Him. He will be first and last and best in everything to us. He will be a present help in every time of need. In these last days of service we shall . . . be held, and led, and protected, by the power of Christ. May the Lord bless and strengthen you, that your last days may be your best days, fragrant with the softening, subduing influence of His love. The Lord bless and keep you and give you repose in His love, is my most earnest desire for you, my brother.—Letter 70, 1898.

Remarriage of S. N. Haskell. We received Brother Haskell's* letter the evening after the Sabbath. We were glad to hear from you that your interests are united as one. May the Lord bless this union, that you may be a strength and support to one another at all times. May the peace of God rest upon you, is my sincere desire and earnest prayer. "Go, stand and speak . . . to the people all the words of this life" [Acts 5:20].

I am pleased, Brother Haskell, that you have a helper [Mrs. Haskell]. This is that which I have desired for some time. The work in which we are engaged has made us one in Christ Jesus to diffuse the knowledge of Jesus Christ. It is your privilege to have happiness in your new relation to each other, in ministering the gospel to those who are in darkness and error. We can sympathize and unite in the grand work that you and I love, and which is the one great object ever before us, the enlargement of the kingdom of Christ and the celebration of His glory. In everything which relates to this we are united in bonds of Christian fellowship, in companionship with heavenly intelligences. . . .

Because of the light given me, I am fully possessed with the conviction that through your united agencies, as sanctified instrumentalities, light shall be reflected to the

---

*Elder S. N. Haskell's first wife died in 1894. This letter refers to his second marriage, which took place in 1897, when he was 64 years old.

salvation of many souls that are now in darkness and error. I know you have not lived unto yourselves but unto Him whom you love and whom you serve and worship.—Letter 74a, 1897.

Advice to J. N. Andrews. I advised you to marry before you returned the last time to Europe for these reasons. First, you needed a wife to care for you and [you] should not have taken your family to Europe without a good companion to be a mother to your children, that these children might not in all things bear the stamp of your mind and be molded according to your ideas. Your mind is not equally balanced. You need another element brought into your labors that you do not possess and that you do not understand is really essential. . . .

Your ideas have been erroneous to preserve your life as a widower, but on this point I will say no more. The influence of a noble Christian woman of proper capabilities would have served to counteract the tendencies of your mind. The ability of concentrativeness, the intense light in which you view everything of a religious character connected with the cause and work of God, has brought upon you depression of spirits, a weight of anxiety that has weakened you physically and mentally. If you had been connected with one who would have opposite feelings, who would have ability to turn your thoughts away from gloomy subjects, who would not have yielded her individuality, but have preserved her identity and had a molding influence upon your mind, you would today have had physical strength and power to resist disease.—Letter 9, 1883.

You remember I wrote you from Texas to obtain a wife before you returned to Europe. Do you suppose I would have given you such advice if I had had no light upon the matter? Be assured, no such counsel would have been given you without good reason. I was shown [that] you follow your own judgment and your own ideas altogether too tenaciously. If you were more willing to be counseled by those you should confide in, and trust less to your own feelings and impressions, the result for yourself and for the cause of God would be far better.

I was shown that you made a mistake in starting to Europe without a companion. If you had, before starting, selected you a godly woman who could have been a mother to your children, you would have done a wise thing, and your usefulness would have been tenfold to what it has been.—Letter 1, 1883.

*A Son's Interference.** I beg of you not to reproach your father. You should not feel as you do, for your father has done nothing that God condemns. His condemnation exists only in the minds of men. He has in no wise dishonored his children. He is keeping the way of the Lord, to do justice and judgment. The Lord is opening the way before him, that he may do a great and good work for His people. Christ is his Saviour, and in beholding Christ he will be changed into His image.

Your father has been a kind, tender husband. For many years he served faithfully her whom he has always loved. Death separated him from the one who for so long has been his special charge. Then his sister was taken from him, and his home was broken up. Is it any wonder that under these

---

*This letter was written July 28, 1902, to the son of Elder George I. Butler, former president of the General Conference. Elder Butler's wife died November 15, 1901, leaving him a widower at the age of 68. As a result of his son's influence, Elder Butler did not marry the woman referred to in this letter. Five years later, in 1907, he married someone else.

circumstances he should, after your mother's death, become attached to a woman in whose conversion to the truth he was instrumental? This woman is not young, but of an age to be a help to him in his work. Should your father's age have stood as a barrier to his happiness? . . .

Had your father married this lady, I believe that the Lord would greatly have blessed them both. But I do not think, seeing that the matter has been treated as it has, it will go any further. Those who refused to sanction this union should remember that one day they must meet the result of their action. But I must leave this matter with those who have been acting a part in it.— Letter 117, 1902.

When Ages Widely Differ. Another cause of the deficiency of the present generation in physical strength and moral worth, is, men and women uniting in marriage whose ages widely differ. It is frequently the case that old men choose to marry young wives. By thus doing, the life of the husband has often been prolonged, while the wife has had to feel the want of that vitality which she has imparted to her aged husband. It has not been the duty of any woman to sacrifice life and health, even if she did love one so much older than herself, and felt willing on her part to make such a sacrifice. She should have restrained her affections. She had considerations higher than her own interest to consult. She should consider, if children be born to them, what would be their condition? It is still worse for young men to marry women considerably older than themselves. The offspring of such unions in many cases, where ages widely differ, have not well-balanced minds. They have been deficient also in physical strength. In such families have frequently been manifested varied, peculiar, and often painful, traits of character. They often die prematurely, and those who reach maturity, in many cases, are deficient in physical and mental strength, and moral worth.

The father is seldom prepared, with his failing faculties, to properly bring up his young family.—2SM 423, 424.

Need of Sound Judgment. Dear Sister: I have just received a letter from Charles B, a student in the school at Lodi, California, pleading with me to inquire of the Lord concerning his mother, whom he says is thinking of marrying a young man many years younger than herself.

I am surprised to hear that a mother forty-six years of age will imperil her happiness, her welfare, and her influence by marrying a young man of twenty. This is a strange matter, and reveals lack of sound judgment. The Lord would have this sister consider carefully the sure result of such a course of action.

In this matter, our sister must be under a strange influence—an influence contrary to the guidance of the Holy Spirit. As the mother of three children, she should feel her accountability to God to move discreetly in all respects, that she may hold her influence over her children, and not pursue any course that they and many others would regard as so questionable. She should realize that her duty to her God and to her children demands the most serious consideration.

My sister, the Lord is not in this matter. Such a marriage would bring strange results—results that would destroy the influence that a mother should earnestly seek to maintain over her own children. This influence I entreat of you to guard sacredly. God has solemnly charged you, as the mother of your children, to bring them up in the nurture and admonition of the Lord. For you at this time to take a youth of twenty as your husband would be strangely inconsistent with your responsibilities as a mother of three sons now grown to manhood.

In the night season I was talking with you concerning these matters, and setting before you the inconsistency of the course under contemplation. I advise you to exercise your ingenuity of mind in an effort to help your children to understand the advantages of loving the Word of God. Show your children that you are cooperating with the Lord in an effort to save their souls.

In the night season it was presented before me that if you should take this strange step, the enemy of all righteousness would use this as a means of ruining the respect that your children would otherwise have for you, and would create in their hearts a feeling of contempt for you because of your lack of good judgment. Satan is seeking to destroy your influence in the home and in the church, and among unbelievers as well.

In past years we have had opportunity to observe several marriages of this sort, and the results have always been of a character to create great misery in the family life.

Now, my sister, I appeal to you to act like a woman of superior judgment. Do, I beseech of you, preserve every jot of your influence, in order that you may use it to the glory of God in giving wise counsel to your own children. You are held accountable before God for the good influence you may now have the power of exerting. For your own sake, and for the sake of your children, cut this matter short.

In the night season I was saying, Give your children, as a true mother, an example of living faith in God, and thus retain the respect and confidence that otherwise you might forever lose.—Letter 26, 1910.

Section II

MARRIED TO AN UNBELIEVING SPOUSE

5. The Christian Spouse's Behavior

No Thought of Divorce. If the wife is an unbeliever and an opposer, the husband cannot, in view of the law of God, put her away on this ground alone. In order to be in harmony with the law of Jehovah, he must abide with her, unless she chooses of herself to depart.—Letter 8, 1888.

*A Christian Wife's Obligations.** I have to tell you something from the Lord. . . . The Lord has a work for you to do; it is not a public work, but a very important one, a work in your own home, to be true to your position as a wife and mother. No other can do this, your work.

The Spirit and the Word of God agree. Remembering this, let us read the words of inspiration from Jesus Christ through Paul to Titus. He is charged to speak "the things which become sound doctrine: that the aged men be sober, grave, temperate, sound in faith, in charity, in patience. The aged women likewise, that they be in behavior as becometh holiness, not false accusers, not given to much wine, teachers of good things: that they may teach the young women to be sober, to love their husbands, to love their children, to be discreet, chaste, keepers at home, good,

---

*Written to a wife who, because of serious abuse by her godless husband, had decided to leave her family and do missionary work.

obedient to their own husbands, that the word of God be not blasphemed'' [Titus 2:1-5].

A Wife's First Duty — Her Home. With this Scripture before you, I ask, For what are you spending your time in Battle Creek? Has God called you to neglect your home? No, no. My sister, the Lord has shown me that you are mistaking your duty. Your husband needs you; your children need their mother. You have stepped out of the path where Jesus leads the way. He is saying to you, "Follow Me," and He will lead you in your own home duties, which are now sadly neglected. The voice of the Lord has not bidden you to separate your interests from that of your husband and children. Your first duty is in the home. The Spirit of the Lord has not given you a work, or qualified you to do a work, that is contrary to His own Word. . . .

Counsel to a Mother. You have a great work, a sacred, holy calling to exemplify the Christian graces as a faithful wife and mother; to be lovable, patient, kind, yet firm, in your home life; to learn right methods and acquire tact for the training of your own little ones, that they may keep the way of the Lord. As a humble child of God, learn in the school of Christ; seek constantly to improve your powers to do the most perfect, thorough work at home, both by precept and example.

In this work you will have the help of the Lord; but if you ignore your duty as a wife and mother, and hold out your hands for the Lord to put another class of work in them, be sure that He will not contradict Himself; He points you to the duty you have to do at home. If you have the idea that some work greater and holier than this has been entrusted to you, you are under a deception. In neglecting your husband and children for what you suppose to be religious duties, either to attend meetings or to work for others, to give Bible readings or to have messages for others, you are going directly contrary to the words of inspiration in the instruction of Paul to Titus. The religion of Christ never leads a wife and mother to do as you have done.

You may now cultivate the home-making qualities with good effect, for your children are of the age when they most need a mother. The restless spirit naturally inclines to mischief; the active mind, if left unoccupied with better things, will give heed to that which Satan may suggest. The children need the watchful eye of the mother. They need to be instructed, to be guided in safe paths, to be kept from vice, to be won by kindness, and be confirmed in well doing, by diligent training.

The Saviour discerns a value and dignity in every soul, because of the image of God which it bears. He died that your children might have the gift of eternal life. He looks upon them with divine compassion. Their souls may be saved unto eternal life, and they are just as precious as the souls of others. The Lord has not called you to neglect your home and your husband and children. He never works in this way, and He never will. You have before your own door a little plot of ground to care for, and God will hold you responsible for this work which He has left in your hands. Through earnest prayer and study, you may become wise in your home, learning the different dispositions of your children and carefully noting their behavior. You may have at home a little school, of which you shall be the teacher. If you seek wisdom from the Lord to understand His way, and to keep it, He will lead you, not away from your home, but back to it.

Poverty No Sin. If you are one of those who are the light of the world, that light is to shine in your home. Poverty has been your lot, but this you could not help, and it was not sin. But your mind has been of that cast which has led you to view everything in too intense a light. Here you have lessons to learn at the feet of Jesus; you need to trust more to Jesus, and be less anxious; you need to have genuine faith in the promises of God. Yet you are to be a laborer together with God, cultivating your mind, that you may bring to the education and training of your children a restful spirit, a loving heart, that you may imbue them with pure aspirations, [and] cultivate in them a love for things honest and pure and holy.

God's Care for Children. Never for a moment suppose that God has given you a work that will necessitate a separation from your precious little flock. Do not leave them to become demoralized by improper associations and to harden their hearts against their mother. This is letting your light shine in a wrong way altogether. You are making it more difficult for your children to become what God would have them and win heaven at last. God cares for them, and so must you if you claim to be His child.

In time past you have erred in having too great an anxiety for your children. Your trust has not been fully in God, and you have indulged them more than was for their good. And now you leave them to themselves. What sort of experience is this? Certainly it has not God and truth for its source. You are offending God in claiming to be led by Him and yet neglecting your duty to your children. . . .

Rights of Husband and Children. When we give ourselves unreservedly to the Lord, the simple, commonplace duties of home life will be seen in their true importance, and we shall perform them in accordance with the will of God. Oh, my sister, you may be bound about with poverty, your lot in life may be humble, but Jesus does not forsake you because of this, neither does He lead you to forsake your family for this or for any other cause. God has made you a trustee, a steward, in your home. Seek to educate yourself for this work, and He will be by your side to bless all your endeavors, that by and by, when the reckoning time for the administration of your trust shall come, He may say, "Well done, thou good and faithful servant."

Your husband has rights; your children have rights; and these must not be ignored by you. Whether you have one talent or three or five, God has given you your work. Parents are fearfully neglectful of their home duties. They do not meet the Bible standard. But to those who forsake their homes, their companions, and children, God will not entrust the work of saving souls, for they have proved unfaithful to their holy vows. They have proved unfaithful to sacred responsibilities. God will not entrust to them eternal riches. . . .

The Christian mother's work begins in the home circle, in making her home what it should be, pleasant to her husband, pleasant to her children. These dear ones are in her hands to educate faithfully. . . .

The Mother, God's Agent. Scolding and fretting, gathering clouds and gloom about the soul, will bring only a shadow and discouragement in the home life. Mothers do not half appreciate their possibilities and privileges. They do not seem to understand that they can be in the highest sense missionaries, laborers together with God in aiding their children to build up a symmetrical character. This is the great burden of the work given them of God. The mother is God's agent to Christianize her family. She is to exemplify Bible religion, showing how its influence is to control us in its everyday duties and pleasures, teaching her children that by grace alone can they be saved, through faith, which is the gift of God. This constant teaching as to what Christ is to us and to them; His love, His goodness, His mercy, revealed in the great plan of redemption, will make a hallowed, sacred impress on the heart.—Letter 28, 1890.

Counsel to the Wife of an Unbelieving Husband. We receive many letters soliciting advice. One mother says her husband is an unbeliever. She has children, but they are taught by the father to disrespect the mother. She is deeply burdened for her children. She does not know what course she can pursue. She then expresses her anxiety to do something in the cause of God, and inquires if I think she has a duty to leave her family, if she is convinced she can do no good to them.

I would answer: My sister, I cannot see how you could be clear before the Lord and leave your husband and your children. I cannot think you would feel that you could do this yourself. The trials you may have may be of a very trying character. You may be often pained to the heart because disrespect is shown you, but I am sure that it must be your duty to care for your own children. This is your field where you have your appointed work. It may be rocky and discouraging soil to work, but you have a Companion in all your efforts to do your duty unflinchingly, conscientiously, notwithstanding all the discouraging circumstances. Jesus is your helper. Jesus came into our world to save lost and perishing souls, and you are to consider that in this work you are a laborer together with God.

Home Trials for Jesus' Ear Only. Do not shirk your responsibilities. Be a daily home missionary. Not only teach your children from their babyhood, but train them. Keep a steady, firm hold upon your children. You must not only tell them what to do, but, to the very best of your ability, make their surroundings favorable and sow your precious seed in the love and spirit of Jesus. Because Satan uses the father of your children to counteract your work, do not be discouraged; do not give up the conflict. Do as you wish them to do. Treat your husband with kindness at all times and on all occasions, and bind your children to your heart with the cords of love. This is your work; this is the burden you have to bear. Talk not your home trials to anyone but Jesus; pour them into His ear.

Jesus "came unto His own, and His own received Him not. But as many as received Him, to them gave He power to become the sons of God, even to them that believe on His name: which were born, not of blood, nor of the will of the flesh, nor of the will of man, but of God" [John 1:11-13].

Value of a Christlike Life. Grace is not inherited. A very bad father may have a godly son; a Christian father a profligate son. Let mothers take up the burdens made doubly heavy for them by the course of the head of the household. This makes your work plain, to let your light shine in the household where Satan is at work to secure your children to himself. Shall he have them? Let the missionary spirit rise to the emergency and say, "No, no; my children, although they have a godless father, are the purchase of the blood of Christ. I am their mother. I will seek the Lord in faith, in humility, that He will not only save my children, but [also] their father, to repentance." Talk not and plead not for the sympathy of your husband and your children, but simply live the life of Christ. In words, in spirit, in character, in meekness, in patience and forbearance, in cheerfulness, be a signpost pointing out the way, the path that leads heavenward.

Be a witness for Christ. Exemplify the strength of the Christian's hope, which is cast into that within the veil. Reveal that the anchor holds you under all circumstances. Let your home be made pleasant and cheerful. Jesus—you must rely on Jesus every moment. Draw your strength from Jesus. He will give you that which you ask in sincerity. If you seek Him with your whole heart, He will be found of you.

Home Missionary Work by Mother. God does not call mothers away from home missionary work which will leave their children under the control of influences that are demoralizing and ruinous to the soul. Are not her children in need of missionary labor? Are not her children worth earnest and prayerful effort? Shall she neglect home missionary work for a larger field? Let her try her skill in her own home—take up her appointed, God-given work. If she has utterly failed, it is because she has not had faith or may not have presented the truth and lived the truth as it is in Jesus. Let her, after years of apparent failure, try again other methods, seeking counsel of God. Present His promises on your knees before Him. "If any of you lack wisdom, let him ask of God, that giveth to all men liberally, and upbraideth not; and it shall be given him. But let him ask in faith, nothing wavering" [James 1:5, 6].

Cheerfulness Better Than Complaining. Have you felt your lot was hard, and complained and murmured? Then as you received no help in this line, begin another course of action. Speak kindly; be cheerful. Because you have Jesus as your helper, break forth in songs of praise. When tempted, when reviled, revile not again; and labor with your children while there is one out of Christ. Sow the seed, the living seed, deep into the soil of the heart. Let your words be wisely chosen. Consider yourself as God's appointed missionary, to be the light of your home.

Again I say, It is not like the works of God to call the mother away from her husband and from her children to engage in what she considers higher work. Take right hold of the duties lying directly in your path.

Post of Duty at Home. I am pained when I receive letters from mothers who have children inquiring, "Shall I leave my children to do missionary work?" In the fear and love of God I say, Become a home missionary. Educate yourself in Bible ways and means, that you may be a successful worker in your own home, for, you see, they need to be saved, for they are sinners. Do not forsake your post of duty because of the unpleasantness of it. There are many living martyrs today who suffer in silence, who trust in God when they are abused with the tongue and who are tantalized, who are hurt and wounded by coarse, harsh denunciations, whose lot seems to be to live and to suffer, receiving comfort only from Jesus who is the Source of their strength. Such souls are missionaries. They are Christ's noble ones, and their names are written in the Lamb's Book of Life.

Remember, Jesus knows it all—every sorrow, every grief; He will not leave you to sink, for His arms are beneath you. You may be an enlightenment to a whole neighborhood if you are indeed patient, kind, forbearing. In this, my sister, consider your questions answered.—Ms 9, 1868.

Secure in God's Promises. It is essential for you to put your trust in God. I am sorry that in the place where you live you have so little encouragement in religious lines. There are many who will give you words of sympathy, but they do not bring comfort to the longing, hungry soul, which is bruised and wounded and which needs the healing balm. Never forget that your Saviour lives and reigns. Your grasp on the divine promises must be strong. Human teachers in Christian faith are few.

You may have felt almost discouraged, and may have yielded to the temptation to neglect your religious duties, to shun the cross-bearing life of a Christian; you may have consented to be governed by worldly principles and sentiments; you may have neglected prayer, neglected to confess Christ. If you have done this, do so no more. Remember the words of Christ, "Ye are My witnesses." Your light may have been flickering, but, thank God, it is not too late, even now, to acknowledge the claims the Lord has upon you.

Trust in the Merits of Christ. You are the property of Jesus Christ. He has purchased you at an infinite cost to Himself. His you are by creation and by redemption. Although to you your hope of heaven may be at times uncertain, yet you know in whom to trust. Your hope of heaven is found alone in the merits of Jesus Christ. You may now gain a living experience in the things of God. Looking unto Jesus by faith, trusting in His merits, doubts of His love will vanish as dew before the morning sun.

Steadfast in Surrender to Christ. Let your surrender to God be full and complete; wait not one day or hour. Make the most now of your probationary time, be it longer or shorter. Just as soon as you cast yourself unreservedly upon Jesus Christ, He accepts you. Do not in any way conceal the fact that you have chosen truth and all the inconveniences that this choice will involve. . . .

Never, under any circumstances, even in appearance, consent to leave the path cast up for the ransomed of the Lord to walk in. Be steadfast, immovable to Christian obligations and to your God. . . .

Sabbathkeeping With the Angels. I urge upon you to fulfill your Christian obligations to God. If there is no one within a hundred miles of you who observes the Sabbath, the whole universe of heaven is in sympathy with you. Christ your Saviour and the heavenly angels are round about you. If you will call upon God in every time of need, He will be your helper. Practice the truth in your home. "Ye are My witnesses, saith the Lord."

The Witness of a Christian Mother. But I am not able to write you more. If you love the father of your children, live the life of a Christian at all times and under all circumstances. If you had done this, God would have worked in your behalf. But when you please yourself, and displease your heavenly Father, how can the Lord work in your behalf?

May the Lord help you, my poor, dear, tempted one, to choose the right way just now. May He help you to give your husband and children a testimony that you are a Christian in practice, that you love God, that you love Jesus, who gave His life for you. And as your day is, so shall your strength be. [See Deut. 33:25.]—Letter 76, 1896.

The Winning of a Non-Christian Companion. My sister, your Saviour is a present help in every time of need. Do not distrust Him. Do not take your troubles to human beings; take them to the Lord. You may think that others should sympathize with you in your downcast feelings, but you will sometimes be disappointed. Jesus never disappoints one who comes to Him for help.

Are you one that makes mistakes? Go to Jesus, and ask Him to forgive you, and then believe that He does. "If we confess our sins, He is faithful and just to forgive us our sins, and to cleanse us from all unrighteousness" [1 John 1:9]. Ask the Lord to pardon your errors, then rejoice in Him. It will not help you in the least to keep mourning over your defects. Say, "Lord, I cast my helpless soul on Thee, and Thee alone. I will not worry, because Thou hast said, 'Ask, and ye shall receive.'" Believe that you do receive. Believe that your Saviour is full of compassion, full of tender pity and love. Let not little mishaps trouble you. Small mistakes may be ordered by the Lord to save you from making larger mistakes.

No Argument With Satan. Act your part in helping yourself, as all must do who would be blessed. Believe that Christ helps you. Refuse to speak a word of unbelief. When the enemy tells you that the Lord has forsaken you, tell him that you know He has not, for He declares, "I came not to call the righteous, but sinners to repentance."

Jesus says, "Him that cometh to Me, I will in no wise cast out" [John 6:37]. Then, my sister, dismiss the enemy. Tell him that you will not dishonor God by doubting His mercy, His goodness, His love. Never argue with Satan, for he has wonderful powers of deception. If, when he went to Adam and Eve, they had kept repeating the words of God, saying "He hath said, and I believe His word, I will not distrust Him," they would not have been overcome.

Singing Better Than Bemoaning. Instead of bemoaning your weakness and talking unbelief and feeling that you are hardly used, begin to sing. Talk of the mercy and love of God. To all who labor and are heavy laden Christ gives the invitation, "Come unto Me, . . . and I will give you rest. Take My yoke upon you, and learn of Me; for I am meek and lowly in heart, and ye shall find rest unto your souls. For My yoke is easy, and My burden is light" [Matt. 11:28-30]. This is the lesson that Christ desires you to learn, and in learning it you will find rest.

Gentle Words. When discouraging words are spoken to you, do not reply unless you can return a pleasant answer. When you are tried and tempted by unkind words, do not retaliate. Say to yourself, "I will not disappoint my Saviour." Every man who is a Christian is a gentleman; and every woman who is a Christian is a gentlewoman. The law of kindness is ever on the lips of the Christian woman. She utters no hasty words. To speak gentle words when you feel irritated will bring sunshine into your heart, and will make your path more smooth. A school girl, in answer to a question, said, "Meek people are those who give soft answers to rough questions." Christ says, "Blessed are the meek; for they shall inherit the earth." They will be fit subjects for the kingdom of heaven, because they are willing to be taught.

You say that your husband is not yet converted to the truth. Show him in your life the advantage of taking Christ at His word. By patience, forbearance, and kindness you may win your husband to the Saviour.

Life Not a Romance but a Reality. In the power of God's grace you may obtain most precious victories. You are not to treat your life as a romance, but as a reality. You are to be a laborer together with God in forming a character that He can approve. "Work out your own salvation with fear and trembling." Does the charge end there? No, no, thank God! "For it is God which worketh in you both to will and to do of His good pleasure" [Phil. 2:12, 13].

You are to be a co-worker with Him in the saving of your soul. You are to will to do the will of God. Then do not spend your time and strength in murmuring, in talking unbelief and finding fault with God. Encourage confidence in Him. Speak kindly of Him. Honor Him who "so loved the world, that He gave His only begotten Son, that whosoever believeth in Him should not perish, but have everlasting life" [John 3:16].

Discharge of Home Duties. Be sure to perform your smallest duties in the fear and love of God, with faithfulness and cheerfulness. God declares, "He that is faithful in that which is least is faithful also in much" [Luke 16:10]. Faithfully discharge your home duties, and then leave yourself with God, saying, "I commit the keeping of my soul to Him. I will not take the ordering of my life out of His hands. I will leave myself in His keeping."

Study the life that Christ lived while on this earth. He did not disregard the simplest, smallest duty that fell to Him. Perfection marked all that He did. Look to Jesus for help, and this will enable you to perform your daily duties with the grace and dignity of one who is seeking for a crown of immortal life. . . .

All that God expects of you and all other Christians is that you live out your profession. Show that Christ's word is true, that He can keep human beings from sin. Conform your life to His pure, beautiful, holy life. Obey His commandments. This will bring you practical godliness.

Only One Life. Do not dwell upon the hardships of the Christian life. Do not talk of your trials, for if you do, you will become more and more inclined to complain of God. Talk of the love of Christ, bringing it into your heart and life. Be thankful that the Lord has spared you, that you have not been cut off without having gained a preparation for entrance into the heavenly kingdom, where there is no sin, no sorrow. You have only one life in which to perfect a Christian character. If you reveal the grace of God in your character, if the law of kindness is ever on your lips, if you constantly thank the Lord for His goodness to you, you are preparing to praise Him in the home above.—Letter 72, 1903.

The Husband's Wishes Regarding Food. The day we visited you we appreciated much the bountiful repast prepared for us. But you need to study how to prepare nutritious food in the most simple way. Your husband's wishes regarding the preparation of food should be respected, and still you may study to prepare appetizing dishes in as simple and healthful a way as possible, so that the fine nerves of the brain will not become weakened and paralyzed, making you excitable, nervous, and easily provoked. . . .

My dear sister, you stand in a responsible position in your home. Hold the reins of government with a wise, even hand. Do not allow the members of your family to lose their love and respect for you. Bind them to your heart with the silken cords of love. This you can do if you live close to Jesus. By beholding Him you will be changed into His image, having escaped the corruption that is in the world through lust. God loves you; He loves your husband, and He is seeking to draw him to Himself. He desires to take his attention off mere earthly enterprises, and fix them on the eternal riches.—Letter 145, 1900.

Section III

A MUTILATED SPOUSE*

6. Counsels to Walter and Laura

Binding Nature of the Marriage Vow. January 9, 1888. I had an interview with Brother C. His earnest solicitation prevailed upon me to go with him to St. Helena and have an interview with his wife. . . .

January 11, 1888. I had a long talk with Sister C, showing her that the marriage vow is binding and could not release its claims upon any of the parties who entered into it, save from the cause of adultery, the violation of the marriage bed. We had much profitable talk upon this subject.— Ms 22, 1888.

Is an Oath Nothing? June 8, 1888. I wish to present before you [Laura] some few points. Why do you not regard facts as they are? You two registered an oath that has been recorded upon the record books of heaven by the recording angel, that you would love one another until death does you

---

*When he was still a young man Walter C carried out the action that he felt was suggested in Matthew 19:12, and made himself a eunuch. According to Walter, Laura married him with full knowledge of his condition. However, she eventually divorced him and married someone else. After her remarriage, Walter also married again. The letters in this section reveal Ellen White's earnest endeavor to protect the sanctity of the marriage commitment even in the face of extremely difficult circumstances.

part. Why do you not remember this? Do you so lightly put aside your vows? Should you yield to evil counsel your honor, your oath, your duty? If evil thoughts have come in upon you, if you have had evil advice suggesting your estrangement, is that a reason you should lightly cast aside your oath? Is an oath nothing? Are your own whims everything?

You may say you do not love your husband. Is that a reason you should not try to do so? Is this life so long and of such value to you that you will choose to have your own way and set aside God's law? I see no possible grounds for you to obtain a divorce. If your husband deceived you, even so, there is your oath. If he told you, as he says he did do, and denies that he deceived you, then you married him, how can you obtain a divorce? I wish you would pursue a course in accordance with the advice I gave you, for I cannot give you any other counsel.

Imperfection No Reason for Dissolving a Marriage. My heart is sick when I see the loose way that the marriage vows are held. We are nearing the judgment. I ask you to consider carefully, candidly, your position. There is, perhaps, upon more thorough acquaintance, a dislike of your husband's ways and manners. Will not many people find the same, after the marriage novelty has passed? But when you made your vow before God and holy angels, you knew you were not perfect and your husband was not perfect; but this is no excuse for breaking your marriage vow. There is a need of training your mind and heart that you shall bear with one another, to be kind to one another, and not to allow distrust and hatred to come in.

Resurrection of Dead Love. I love you, my sister, and I do not want you to take a course to ruin your own happiness and that of your husband. Those who have come in to teach you to do this had better be searching their own hearts. When you bring your will more to your aid, and conscientiously move in the fear of God, then the love you now suppose to be dead will be found to have a resurrection, unless you play upon each other's evil nature and stir up the worst qualities of the human heart. The fountain of love will increase day by day and in time will exclude all bitterness and disappointments.

You know you have kindly feelings toward your husband, for he is your husband and he loves you with all his heart. Your love would be precious to him, a light, an inspiration to his life. Your husband will appreciate your love; he will value it, and it will have a modifying, elevating influence upon his life. You may have fancies and ideas and whims that you may not at once surrender, and your husband may have to bear humbly and patiently with you. But you have noble traits of character that, if not disregarded and abused, will come to your help.

Need of Forbearance. Now, I tell you that you cannot break your marriage vow and be guiltless before God. Unite your interest with your husband. Love him and bear with him and work with him. Bid the evil advisers depart. The case is between you and your husband and your God. It is a pride of heart that shuts your eyes that you cannot and do not discover the justice and righteousness in the case of fidelity to your husband. Adhere faithfully to your marriage vows because you are upright of heart, and will you regret this keeping of your vows when you shall be clothed in the garments of Christ's righteousness?

Perfection Only in Christ. We have only a brief season here upon the earth, a time when licentious practices under the marriage vow are ruining thousands and tens of thousands. While you have some cross to lift, do not, I beg you for Christ's sake, depart from justice and righteousness. Let your lives be in sobriety, and bring your will power into the matter, looking not for perfection in each other, but looking unto Jesus who is the author and finisher of your faith. Strive to run the Christian race with patience, keeping the crown of life in view, seeking to have a knowledge of the will of God, striving for precedence in His acquaintance and affections.

You will, I know, when convinced of the right way, act resolutely, not as a child, but according to your convictions and according to your feelings. Give yourself to God without reserve, soul, body, and spirit. Go to work in the cause of God, doing good, and the Lord will bless you. Do not become self-centered. Think of someone's soul; think of the self-denying, self-sacrificing life of Jesus. Turn your attention away from yourself to Jesus and His life and His character.—Letter 57, 1888.

Acceptance of the Facts. August 29, 1888. I cannot see what more can be done in this case, and I think that the only thing that you [Walter C] can do is to give up your wife. If she is thus determined not to live with you, both she and you would be most miserable to attempt it. And as she has fully and determinedly set her stakes, you can only shoulder your cross and show yourself a man. . . .

I hope you will be a man. Lay aside this matter, go to your labor, do your duty irrespective of everyone else on the earth, self-forgetting, self-denying, self-sacrificing. In this will be your power. Jesus our Redeemer comes to men and says, I love you; I want to make you happy. He shows His hands and His feet and says, I have suffered for your sake; I bear the shafts that are aimed at you; I will carry your burdens; I will shelter you. Trust in My surety and you shall have the great reward of life forevermore.

No Time for Self-pity. I say, put your trust in God. Your mind has been perplexed and occupied with this matter regarding your wife. Now in the name of Jesus lay this matter down; leave your case with the Lord. Let your experience humble you. Christ is with the weak and the tempted and forsaken, to give them His divine sympathy and rest. You need rest of mind. Give up Laura and fasten your affections on God. He will give you relief. Time is short; you have no time to stop and pity yourself; go to work for the Master. Do your duty to the very best of your ability; do not give up to discouragement; walk humbly with God; seek communion with God. Do not let your disappointment make you self-centered, to think of yourself, talk of yourself. . . . Live for God. Be kind, be courteous. Let not this disappointment ruin you. Cast off your melancholy. God will help you if you will be true to Him. Remember, the eye of God is upon you, searching the depths of your soul. . . .

May the Lord help, strengthen, and bless you, to do your best. Look away from earthly things, earthly idols, and worship the Lord thy God, and serve Him with thy whole heart, and with thy whole soul, and then you will be wholly devoted to the Lord.—Letter 40, 1888.

Disregard of Light. I hoped to meet you [Laura] and talk with you. I greatly fear that you disregard the light which the Lord has been pleased to give you through me. I know that the Lord has tender, pitying love toward you, and I hope you will not under temptation be led to pursue a course to separate your soul from God. There are many who are ready to give advice and confuse the mind with counsel, who have not God for their counselor; therefore all they may say will only make a mixed case of one that is already very trying.

My sister, your disposition and temperament are such that I greatly fear for your soul. I fear that you will not choose for your companions those who are discreet and wise and humble in heart, who love God and who keep His commandments.

Satan's Battle for the Soul. We read that Satan has come down in great wrath, working with his deceiving power upon the hearts and minds of all who listen to his suggestions. You know something of the love of God; you know something of the peace of Christ; and Satan is at work playing the game of life for your soul. Shall he be victor? Will he gain his purpose? God forbid.

The Lord has been giving you light, but you have not walked in it. Are you satisfied in pursuing the course which you are pursuing? Your own way, your will, is not the best for you to follow. I am sure that Satan is trying to secure you to himself. Shall he do it? Will you choose to go your own way in the place of keeping the way of the Lord? Will you place yourself upon the enemy's ground?

Avoid Even the Appearance of Evil. Abstain from even the appearance of evil, is the exhortation of the inspired apostle. Have you done this? With your temperament this is most difficult for you to do while you are traveling from place to place canvassing. Do you feel, my sister, that you are moving conscientiously? Are you not having in your character a one-sided development? Are not traits of character [which are] not the most desirable strengthening, which will mar your future life? The sensational and emotional are more fully developed than the intellectual. Everything, my sister, should be avoided that would exaggerate this tendency into a predominating power. You have motive power; let it be uncorrupted and wholly devoted to God. God has bestowed upon you capabilities and powers to be sanctified and exercised to His glory.

You have a history, and you are making history. The mind may in this crisis of your life take a turn, a bias of grossness rather than of refinement. The contaminating influences of the world may mold your habits, your taste, your conversation, your deportment. You are on the losing side. The precious moments, so solemn, fraught with eternal results, may be wholly on Satan's side of the question, and may prove your ruin. I do not want it thus. I want you to be a Christian, a child of God, an heir of heaven.

Importance of Parental Counsel. You have been giving the complexion to your life. How stands your case as registered in heaven's record book? Above everything else seek for those things which make for your peace. Place yourself under influences which will not be deteriorating, destroying the fine sensibility of the soul. Keep your soul unspotted from the world. Let not any familiarity with young men put a blot on your life. You are in danger of giving up Christ, of becoming reckless and unwilling to listen to wise counsel. The counsel of parental affection is lost upon deaf ears. Will you, my sister, think seriously whether you will receive advice from the experienced? Will you be guided by your friends? Will the parental counsel be unheeded? Will you take your case in your own hands?

Retracing One's Steps. I hope you will change your course of action, for if the Lord has ever spoken by me, He now speaks to you to retrace your steps. Your passions are strong; your principles are endangered; and you will not consider and will not follow advice which you know to be good and the only clear, safe, consistent thing for you to do. Will you resolve to do right, to be right, to heed the counsel

I have given you in the name of the Lord? God has given you capabilities. Shall they be wasted at random? Unguided efforts will go more often in the wrong direction than the right. Will you let years of waywardness, disappointment, and shame pass, and you make so many wrong impressions on minds by your course of action that you can never have that influence which you might have had?

Your course of life has been of that character that all your good is evil spoken of. You become soured, unsanctified, and unholy. In order to gain that which you think is liberty you pursue a course which, if followed, will hold you in a bondage worse than slavery. You must change your course of conduct and be guided by the counsel of experience, and, through the wisdom of those whom the Lord teaches, place your will on the side of the will of God.

Stain on the Soul. But if you are determined to listen to no counsels but your own, and you will work out every problem for yourself, then be sure you will reap that which you have sown. You will miss the right way altogether or else, wounded, bruised, and dwarfed in religious character, you will turn to the Lord, humbled, penitent, and confessing your errors. You will become tired of beating the air.

Are you sure that your course is right? I know you are not; but pride has taken possession of your soul. You are too giddy or too reckless to take counsel. Remember, every action and every course of action has a twofold character, be it virtuous or demoralizing. God is displeased with you. Can you afford to pursue the course you are pursuing? A stain is being imprinted upon your soul.—Letter 47, 1889.

Like Clay in Jesus' Hands. I beg of you, Laura, to go to God for wisdom. The most difficult thing you will have to manage is your own self. Your own daily trials, your emo-

tions, and your peculiar temperament, your inward prompt-
ings, these are difficult matters for you to control, and these
wayward inclinations bring you often into bondage and
darkness. Your only course is to give yourself unreservedly
into the hands of Jesus—all your experiences, all your
temptations, all your trials, all your impulses—and let the
Lord mold you as clay is molded in the hands of the potter.
You are not your own, therefore the necessity of giving
your unmanageable self into the hands of One who is able
to manage you; then rest, precious rest and peace, will come
to your soul. Lie passive in the hands of God.

Pictures in Heaven's Record Books. Remember, your
character is being daguerreotyped [photographed] by the
great Master Artist in the record books of heaven, as
minutely as the face is reproduced upon the polished plate
of the artist. What do the books of heaven say in your case?
Are you conforming your character to the Pattern, Jesus
Christ? Are you washing your robes of character and
making them white in the blood of the Lamb? "Behold, I
come quickly; and My reward is with Me, to give every
man according as his work shall be" [Rev. 22:12]. . . .

Changing Before It is Too Late. Laura, it is not now too
late for wrongs to be righted. It is not now too late to make
your calling and your election sure. You may now begin to
work upon the plan of addition. Add to your faith virtue,
and knowledge, and temperance, and patience, and every
Christian grace. Everything else will perish in the great day
of conflagration, but the gold of holy character is enduring.
It knows no decay. It will stand the test of the fires of the
last day. My dear child, I wish you to remember that "God
shall bring every work into judgment, with every secret
thing, whether it be good, or whether it be evil" [Eccl.
12:14].

Truth is unfolding to those who walk in the light of the sun of Christ's righteousness. The truth sanctifies. We see vice prevailing everywhere. It is pampered and glorified, while true goodness, equity, justice, and purity are trampled underfoot. A large number are sowing seeds of baleful influence around them. What are you doing, Laura? Have you, since you decided to discard counsel, to refuse advice, been growing into a firm, well-developed Christian, or have you, in choosing your own way, found it brings unrest, cares, and worries?

Life's Most Crucial Choice. Why not listen to the advice of your parents? Before you is the path that leads to certain ruin. Will you turn while you can? Will you seek the Lord while Mercy's sweet voice is appealing to you, or will you still have your own way? The Lord pities you. The Lord invites you. Will you come? Will you return from your backslidings? May the Lord help you to choose to be wholly the Lord's.—Letter 51, 1889.

One's Own Counsel and Will. Dear Sister Laura: I thought I would write you a few lines because I have interest in your soul, and I am sure your feet have been dangerously long in the path that leads to perdition. You have not been gaining any strength to overcome every defect of character, but you have been pursuing a course that is unchristian. Now, I know that had you followed the advice which I gave you in the name of the Lord, you would today be far in advance of what you now are spiritually. But all my advice was cast aside as naught, and I felt that it was no use to seek to do you good because my soul would be wounded and your soul unhelped, unless I should coincide with your ideas in regard to your marriage with Walter. This I shall never do because I know you are pursuing a course which is not right, and which the Lord will not approve. If your course were right, you would not have suffered as you have.

Your course since you left Walter has been such as has not raised you in the estimation of anyone who has the love of God abiding in the heart. You have ever loved to be in the society, and have encouraged the attention, of young men. This you have done to your own injury. Advice and counsel in this matter have not done you any good, but created in you feelings of resentment. But will you consider how the heavenly angels look upon the course you have persistently pursued in having your own way, and your own will, strong, defiant, determined?

Reflections in God's Mirror. You have kept to your own ideas irrespective of right or righteousness. Does it pay, Laura? Can you afford to spend the few moments of probation in the kind of life you have chosen? Certainly had you consented to live with Walter, you would not have been any more unhappy than you have been. You have set up your will, but is it God's will? But I wish you to see yourself as God sees you. You once loved God, but you have lost your first love. You do not love God; you do not love holy things. Your influence is not to others a savor of life unto life, but of death unto death. In the place of growing in grace and the knowledge of our Lord and Saviour Jesus Christ, you are separating farther and farther from the Lord.

Spiritual Coldness and Declension. If you were pursuing a right course, you would not reveal this spiritual declension. The Bible is not precious to you as it once was. You read it a little out of a sense of duty, but not because you wish to hear the voice of God in His Word. You pray sometimes, but it is only a form. You do not take all your troubles to God and plead with an humble heart to know

His ways and His will. We cannot sanction your course; we have not felt that your example was safe for anyone to follow.

In the place of widening the mark that separates you from the world, you have been narrowing the mark until it is obliterated. Should the Lord say today, Cut down the tree; why cumbereth it the ground? you would have no part in the first resurrection. Your conversation is not refined and choice; no one would suppose you to be a Christian by your loose, reckless talk, and the company you have chosen of late years. You are losing and so is your sister every day, making it harder and more difficult for you to retrace your steps.

Entirely Reckless and Careless? Can you afford to do this? Have you become entirely reckless and careless in regard to your soul? I have a message from God to you that you need not despair, but return unto the Lord. ''Seek the Lord while He may be found, call ye upon Him while He is near: let the wicked forsake his way, and the unrighteous man his thoughts: and let him return unto the Lord, and He will have mercy upon him; and to our God, for He will abundantly pardon'' (Isa. 55:6, 7).

Lose sight of everything but one thing, that is, How is it with my soul? Should sickness and sudden death come to me now, what is my hope of entering the mansions Jesus has gone to prepare for those who love Him? Shall Jesus have died for me in vain? Will you choose your way, your will, and refuse to keep the way of the Lord?

Need of a Return to God. Your heart has been growing harder and harder, but, Laura, fall on the Rock and be broken; surrender yourself to God; return to Jesus. The same sunshine that once shone into your heart and melted it, the same sunbeams of the Sun of Righteousness that illuminated your mind with their pure rays, are seeking your heart and mind today. The same Jesus who spoke pardon to your soul is speaking to you today. His blood has lost none of its efficacy; it can cleanse you from all sin. The same Spirit that once drew you to Jesus with the cords of His love, is waiting to lead you back to Him again. Do not think of anything except it is Jesus. Break your heart, confess your sins, forsake them and turn to the Lord with full purpose of heart. When you show a determination to be right before God, to forsake your way for God's way, then will He restore unto you His salvation.

Weakened Will Power. Some things that look impossible to you now will certainly change in appearance when your heart is changed by the grace of God. Your heart has become sad at times as you know you are in an unsaved state and that you are grieving the Saviour by your wrong doings. When you come to yourself you are amazed at the distance you have placed between yourself and your Saviour. You have again and again resolved to reform, but you have as often failed because you made these resolutions in your own strength. Your moral power has become weak. Your will power is strong enough, but it is not strong on the Lord's side. You are not able to fix your mind upon the Word of God. You have talked enough, but it has only sunk you lower. Your heart does not feel when you try to pray.

The Sinner's Cry. Now make a desperate effort. Take your mind off from yourself, off from your securing a divorce, off from Walter, off from everything mortal; and commence with your own soul. Cry out in earnest, Lead me to the Rock that is higher than I; save, Lord, or I perish. "Create in me a clean heart, O God; and renew a right spirit within me. . . . Purge me with hyssop, and I shall be clean: wash me, and I shall be whiter than snow" (Ps. 51:10, 7).

We are surrounded with iniquity in its various forms. You need a helper. The Lord knows all our works; even our thoughts are before Him as an open book. I now make my appeal to you. It is to change right about. Step from under Satan's hellish banner, and step under the blood-stained banner of Jesus Christ. Will you do this? Will you change your spirit for the spirit of Christ? When your mind delights to dwell upon heaven and heavenly things, there will be no desire with you to enjoy the society of young men. There will be kindled in the soul the most intense desire to be like Jesus. By beholding we become changed into the same image. Carnal thoughts, carnal feelings, will be no longer entertained. You will no longer be frivolous, cheap in talk, and unholy in life. Then you will reach, through the grace of Christ, the highest standard of purity and elevation of character.

I now commit you to God and to His grace. But work out your own salvation with fear and trembling, for it is God who worketh in you both to will and to do of His good pleasure.—Letter 14a, 1891.

7. Admonition to Walter's Second Mother-in-law

Dear Sister:* In regard to the marriage of your daughter with Walter C, I see where you are troubled. But the marriage took place with your consent, and your daughter, knowing all about him, accepted him as her husband; and now I can see no reason why you should carry any burden over this matter. Your daughter loves Walter C, and it may be that this marriage is in the order of God in order that both Walter and your daughter may have a richer Christian experience and be built up where they are deficient. Your

_____
*Written August 26, 1895, to the mother of Walter C's second wife.

daughter has pledged herself to Walter C in marriage, and to break her marriage vows would be far from right. She cannot now disannul her obligations to him.

You say that Walter was engaged to some young lady in Topeka. I cannot speak concerning this, for I have not heard Walter's reasons for breaking his engagement, if he did so. But I had a personal knowledge of his former relations with his first wife, Laura. Walter loved Laura far too well, for she was not worthy of his regard. He did all in his power to help her, and sought in every possible way to retain her as his wife. He could not have done more than he did do. I pleaded with her, and tried to show her the inconsistency of her course, and begged her not to obtain a divorce; but she was determined and willful and stubborn, and would have her own way. While she lived with him she sought to secure all the money possible from him, but she would not treat him kindly as a wife should treat her husband.

A Right to Happiness. Walter did not put his wife away. She left him, and put him away, and married another man. I see nothing in the Scripture that forbids him to marry again in the Lord. He has a right to the affection of a woman who, knowing his physical defect, shall choose to give him her love. The time has come when a sterile condition is not the worst condition to be in. I see wives who have borne large families of children, and they are unable to give them proper care. These women do not have time to recover from the weakness of bearing one child before they are with child again.

Many of these women are the wives of poor men who have not sufficient means to support their increasing families, and I am at the present time helping them to feed and clothe and educate their children. But notwithstanding their inability to support their offspring, children are brought into the world as fast as possible. But God is not in this kind of doing.

The husbands of these women seem to think that their wives are for no other purpose than to gratify their lustful passions. Children are brought into the world so rapidly, responsibilities accumulate so speedily, that the wives and mothers have no chance for the cultivation of their minds, no time or opportunity to devote to religious work. God is not glorified in such families.

Many of our young women missionaries marry, and in a few months' time they have children to care for and are taken out of the missionary field. You may rejoice that your daughter will not be thus hindered in her work for the Master. She can accompany her husband in his travels and be a help to him, and when she is left at home she can work for the Lord as though she were unmarried. This is my view of the matter.

I have confidence in Walter and believe that he is a Christian. I had occasion to know something of the temper of his spirit when he was going through his trial with his first wife. She tried to extract money from him when she saw she had the advantage of him, and he was willing to do tenfold more for her than it was her right to expect, or his duty to do. He had sore and hard trials on her account. I have tried to help him all that I could.

I have tried to enable Laura to see and understand her duty. But as she has taken the course that she has, I cannot see that this new union should be disturbed. It is a serious matter to part a man and his wife. There is no Scriptural ground upon which to take such a step in this case. He did not leave her, she left him. He did not marry again until she had obtained a divorce. When Laura divorced herself from Walter he suffered most keenly, and it was not until Laura had married another man that Walter married again. The one he has chosen, I feel certain, will be a help to him, and he can be a help to her.

Walter is not perfect in character. He has some objectionable characteristics. He has been entrusted with means, and he does not always put it to the very best account. Sometimes he is very lavish of his money, and sometimes very narrow in its use, and severely economical. But a good God-fearing woman at his side will be able to advise him not to move impulsively, and counsel him to place his money in the treasury of the Lord.

Walter is in a responsible position, but if the members of the family to which he has allied himself in marriage will prove true to him, they will influence him to become a wise steward of his Lord's goods. Then he will bestow his means as if in the view of the whole universe of heaven. He will not participate in any unlawful scheme for making money but will move with an eye single to the glory of God. He will eschew all petty tricks and avoid all mean, dishonest devices, and will do nothing that will [in] any way work against the cultivation of true piety. He will realize that all his business transactions lie within the domain of God.

We must not lose sight of the fact that the steward is to trade with his Lord's goods, and that he is handling a sacred responsibility. The Bible requires that men buy and sell and transact all their business with as keen a sense of their religious obligation as they have when offering up petitions to their heavenly Father, asking for strength and grace. The Lord has not left anyone to do as he pleases with his goods, and to give as impulse shall dictate, or as friends may demand. The money he handles is not his, and is not to be expended unnecessarily, for the vineyard of the Lord is to be worked, and its working requires the expenditure of means.

Now is our day of trust, and the day of reckoning is yet to come. The Lord has entrusted means to His stewards to be used wisely, for all are moral agents and are required to bear responsibilities. Our varied trusts are given in proportion to our ability to use, but we are not to use God's means merely for the gratification of selfish desires, and as inclination may dictate.

Walter C has failed at times in the past in handling his Lord's goods, and has not always considered whether he was using the money entrusted to him in a way that would please his Master and advance the cause of truth. He must give an account of how he disposes of the means given in trust to him. He cannot study his own will in this matter. He must seek wisdom from God. I do not desire Walter to bestow one dollar in this destitute field unwillingly, for unwilling offerings are not accompanied with the blessing of God. I have no urging to do and do not wish to force money from anyone even for the work of God.

God has a work to do, and I am using all the means that I can spare, and provide myself with home, livelihood, and common conveniences. There are others who gladly and willingly help me in this part of the Lord's vineyard. If all do their duty according to the measure of their responsibilities, the amount entrusted to them will be doubled. He who gives back to God His own will be honored for his fidelity and will hear the Master say, "Well done, thou good and faithful servant." But it is not proper for persons to give just as the notion may strike them. Christ has a right to all that we have.

You must not be surprised that Walter does not feel free to help your son. If your son has not appreciated the opportunities and privileges he has had, if he has misapplied his own powers, and wasted his God-given talents, the question is, will he do better upon a second trial? Has he learned the lesson that God wills he should learn? There are many precious souls who would be so glad of a chance to obtain an education, who will not sow wild oats, but will use every capability in obtaining knowledge with which to do good.

I am surprised that Walter did not at once accede to your request, as you were the mother of his wife whom he loves. It may be that he is learning caution, and is taking the lesson of the past to heart. He has helped many whom it was not his duty to help. You should take his refusal to give you money as an evidence of his sincerity in that he will not compromise himself to win your favor. I am sure that Walter means to do his duty. The mistakes he made in bestowing his money on his first wife's family have probably taught him not to repeat the experiment. I hope that his refusal to give you means to enable your son to go to Battle Creek or to Union College will not cause you to become prejudiced against him. It should have no such influence.

If your daughter loves Walter C, I see nothing in the Word of God that would require her to separate from him. As you have asked my advice, I will freely give it to you. If Walter had given you the money you asked for, would it not have been something like trying to buy your favor? Would it not be much more fitting for your son to go to work and secure money for himself, and educate himself, rather than to be dependent upon anybody for such a favor? There is such a thing as giving unwise help to our children.

Those who work their way through college appreciate their advantages more than those who are provided with them at someone else's expense, for they know their cost. We must not carry our children until they become helpless burdens. Educate your son to be diligent, able to sustain himself, and to help others.

God is the proprietor of the universe. Every man, woman, and child, with all the time and talents that have been bestowed upon them, belongs to God. He has given ability to men that they may use it to His glory and thus have increased ability, wisdom, and understanding. God has a claim upon every soul, and we are responsible agents, and should give Him constant service. Body, soul, and spirit, we should consecrate ourselves to His service, and do those things that will forward His cause in the earth. We are to do His will upon the earth. Our pleasure is not to be consulted, nor permitted to be the governing impulse.

Now, my dear sister, I will send you this letter, and also forward a copy of it to Walter C. I desire to act the part of a mother to him. In times of affliction he has needed a mother. Every penny he has placed in my hands has been used for the saving of perishing souls, and in time to come may it be his experience to hear from the lips of the Master, "Well done, thou good and faithful servant, enter thou into the joy of thy Lord."

I am truly sorry that you have taken upon yourself unnecessary burdens. Do you not see that in separating Walter and your daughter, you would create two evils instead of curing one? Your daughter has married Walter, and there is no reason why she should be separated from him. You have no just excuse for desiring them to cease living and working together as man and wife. You may give publicity to the evil reports that may come to you, and be the means of making yourself, your daughter, and her husband miserable. Let these two, as children of God, unite their interests as their marriage vows require them to do, let them consecrate themselves to God to do His will, to be vessels unto honor, meet for the Master's use.

On your part, act as a faithful mother should. Be wise to

counsel and help them in every way that lies in your power. Knowing that you all belong to God, deal justly and lovingly with each other. Be frank, be kind, cultivate whole-souled integrity, and you will win a crown of life that fadeth not away. Have perfect trust in God, and He will bless you, and give you peace and rest.—Letter 50, 1895.

8. Failure of Walter's Second Marriage*

To the Second Mrs. C. April 16, 1907. Dear Sister C: I have received your letter, and in reply to it I would say, I cannot advise you to return to Walter C unless you see decided changes in him. The Lord is not pleased with the ideas he has had in the past of what is due to a wife. At one time I spoke very plainly to Walter in regard to his responsibilities to his wife. It is very clear to me that it would be a mistake for you to be united again while your love for him is quenched. He cannot make you happy unless his views are changed.

----

*Concerning Walter C's second marriage, W. C. White states: "Fear took hold of him that his new wife would want some of his money with which to help her relatives, so he labored for some years to separate her as much as possible from her relatives. Bringing her to California he made no move toward providing a home, but was pleased to have her take the nurses' course at the St. Helena Sanitarium. When she had advanced sufficiently in this course so as to earn something, he permitted her to work her own way with very limited assistance financially from him. . . .

"For years he has placed money in Mother's hands to be used as she thought best for the advancement of the cause. Sometimes she has felt that a portion of this money ought to be given to Mrs. C, but when C learned that a part of the money which he placed in Mother's hands had been given by Mother to his wife, he gave notice that this was contrary to his wish, and that if any more was used that way he should not feel free to place his gifts in Mother's hands."—White Estate Document File 1002-A.

Responsibility to Parents. You have a duty to perform to your mother. You should not place yourself in a position where you would be miserable and unhappy; and if Brother C holds to his former views, the future would be no better for you than the past has been. He does not know how to treat a wife.

I feel very sad about this matter. I feel indeed sorry for Walter, but I cannot advise you to go to him against your judgment. I speak to you as candidly as I spoke to him; it would be perilous for you to again place yourself under his dictation. I had hoped that he would change.

Brother C can place his father in one of our sanitariums, where he will have good care. Your experience of the past is not to be repeated. When you are released from the care of your mother, you can act a part in one of our sanitariums.

The Lord understands all about your experiences, Sister C. Be of good courage in the Lord; He will not leave you nor forsake you. My heart goes out in tenderest sympathy for you. Hang your helpless soul on Christ.

Help Needed in Sanitarium. You know that not one word passed between you and me in regard to your going to Battle Creek, neither have you spoken to me concerning your life with Brother C in the past. Not a word of complaint have you made to me. The course you took in going to Battle Creek you took on your own responsibility, because you deemed it just and right; and this I do not condemn.

Now, my dear sister, you have obtained a knowledge of how to treat the sick, and your help is needed in our sanitarium work. When you write, please tell me in regard to your mother's health.

What are you doing? We need faithful workers in our sanitariums that can give treatment.—Letter 148, 1907.

Section IV

SEPARATION AND GROUNDS FOR DIVORCE

9. Separation

A Demon-controlled Wife. Dear Brother D: I hoped the change which seemed to take place in your wife at the meeting in Chicago would be lasting, and was so grateful to our heavenly Father when I heard her confession, for I thought that a most severe task was lifted from my shoulders; but the burden is still upon me. I know that she is not changed for the better. The dangers and difficulties which she will create if her whims are gratified, are almost incredible to those who do not understand the spirit which actuates her. . . .

However earnestly her husband may endeavor to pursue a straightforward course to serve God, she will be his evil angel, seeking to lead him away from righteousness. In her own estimation she is the idol he must worship; in fact, she is Satan's agent, seeking to occupy the place where God should be. She has followed the impulses of her own unconsecrated heart until Satan has almost complete control of her. . . .

Unless there is a change, a time will come soon when this lower nature in the wife, controlled by a will as strong as steel, will bring down the strong will of the husband to her own low level. . . . In this case it is not the woman whom Brother D is dealing with, but a desperate, satanic spirit. The Lord has a work for Brother D to do; but if he is

(76)

overcome by these outbursts on the part of his wife, he is a lost man, and she is not saved by the sacrifice.

Separation Better Than Apostasy. His best course with this child-wife, so overbearing, so unyielding, and so uncontrollable, is to take her home, and leave her with the mother who has made her what she is. Though it must be painful, this is the only thing for him to do, if he would not be ruined spiritually, sacrificed to the demon of hysterics and satanic imaginings. Satan takes entire control of her temper and will, and uses them like desolating hail to beat down every obstruction. Her husband can do her no good, but is doing himself incalculable harm, and robbing God of the talents and influence He has given.

God has placed the husband at the head of the family, and until Sister D shall learn her place and duties as a wife, it will be best for him not to be connected with her in any way. The wife is to respect and obey, but if she utterly refuses to keep the marriage vow, she will be more and more the sport of Satan's temptations; and if her husband consents to keep her by his side, to wear out his life, he will become discouraged and unfitted for the Lord's service. He is under no obligations to keep one by his side who will only torture his soul. I was shown that he has already been losing his manhood, and has been influenced and molded by his wife. Their marriage was a snare of Satan.

Priority of God's Claims. Sister D is determined to rule or ruin. I was shown that she has so thoroughly yielded herself into Satan's hands that her husband fears for her reason, but he will make one of the gravest mistakes of his life if he permits himself to be controlled by Satan through the device of his wife. I tell you plainly, she is controlled by demons, and if these evil spirits have their way, your liberty, Brother D, your manhood, is gone; you are a slave to her caprices. . . . She is just as much possessed by a demon as was the man who tore and cut himself when Jesus cast out the devils. . . . Brother D must let Satan rage, and not allow himself to be cut off from religious privileges because his wife desires it.

If she runs away, let her go. Even if she threatens to take her own life, do not yield to her wicked demands. Even if she should carry out her threat, it would be better to look upon her silent in death than to allow her to murder not only her own soul but that of her husband, and be the means of destroying many others.

Permanent Nature of Marriage Vows. Brother D, you have been terrified by the violence of your wife, but the course for you to pursue is the straightforward path of truth, righteousness, and wisdom, having the fear of God always before you. Satan is already exulting over his success.

Sister D, I would not present this matter as I do were there not another life so closely bound up with yours, and the life of one whom God has chosen to be His servant. This marriage ought not to have been, but the step has been taken, and for your husband the work of overcoming is now tenfold more severe than if he had never seen you. Will you think seriously over this question, whether his usefulness shall be destroyed and his life become a failure because of your course? . . . Your husband should not merge his identity in you. The marriage vow that binds the husband to the wife must remain unbroken, but he has vows to his Lord, to love Him with the whole heart, the undivided affection.— Letter 34, 1890.

10. Grounds for Divorce

Adultery the Only Reason for Divorce. A woman may be legally divorced from her husband by the laws of the land

and yet not divorced in the sight of God and according to the higher law. There is only one sin, which is adultery, which can place the husband or wife in a position where they can be free from the marriage vow in the sight of God. Although the laws of the land may grant a divorce, yet they are husband and wife still in the Bible light, according to the laws of God.

I saw that Sister Jones, as yet, has no right to marry another man; but if she, or any other woman, should obtain a divorce legally on the ground that her husband was guilty of adultery, then she is free to be married to whom she chooses.—AH 344.

Among the Jews a man was permitted to put away his wife for the most trivial offenses, and the woman was then at liberty to marry again. This practice led to great wretchedness and sin. In the Sermon on the Mount Jesus declared plainly that there could be no dissolution of the marriage tie except for unfaithfulness to the marriage vow. "Everyone," He said, "that putteth away his wife, saving for the cause of fornication, maketh her an adulteress: and whosoever shall marry her when she is put away committeth adultery" [Matt. 5:32, R.V.].

When the Pharisees afterward questioned Him concerning the lawfulness of divorce, Jesus pointed His hearers back to the marriage institution as ordained at creation. "Because of the hardness of your hearts," He said, Moses "suffered you to put away your wives: but from the beginning it was not so" (Matt. 19:8). He referred them to the blessed days of Eden, when God pronounced all things "very good." Then marriage and the Sabbath had their origin, twin institutions for the glory of God in the benefit of humanity. Then, as the Creator joined the hands of the holy pair in wedlock, saying,

A man shall "leave his father and his mother, and shall cleave unto his wife: and they shall be one" (Gen. 2:24), He enunciated the law of marriage for all the children of Adam to the close of time. That which the Eternal Father Himself had pronounced good was the law of highest blessing and development for man.—MB 63.

Change Disposition, Not the Marriage Status. I have received a letter from your husband. I would say that there is only one thing for which a husband may lawfully separate from his wife or a wife from her husband, and that is adultery.

If your dispositions are not congenial, would it not be for the glory of God for you to change these dispositions?

A husband and wife should cultivate respect and affection for each other. They should guard the spirit, the words, and the actions so that nothing will be said or done to irritate or annoy. Each is to have a care for the other, doing all in their power to strengthen their mutual affection.

I tell you both to seek the Lord. In love and kindness do your duty one to the other. The husband should cultivate industrious habits, doing his best to support his family. This will lead his wife to have respect for him.—AH 345.

Section V

LICENTIOUSNESS AND ADULTERY

11. The Sin of Licentiousness

Rescue From Sin and Impurity. When the law of God is written in the heart, it will be exhibited in a pure and holy life. The commandments of God are no dead letter. They are spirit and life, bringing the imaginations and even the thoughts into subjection to the will of Christ. The heart in which they are written will be kept with all diligence, for out of it are the issues of life.

All who love Jesus and keep the commandments will seek to avoid the very appearance of evil; not because they are constrained thus to do, but because they are copying a pure model, and feel averse to everything contrary to the law written in their hearts. They will not feel self-sufficient, but their trust will be in God, who alone is able to keep them from sin and impurity. The atmosphere surrounding them is pure; they will not corrupt their own souls or the souls of others. It is their pleasure to deal justly, to love mercy, and to walk humbly before God.

Last-day Dangers. The danger that lies before those living in these last days is the absence of pure religion, the absence of heart holiness. The converting power of God has not wrought in transforming their characters. They profess to believe sacred truths, as did the Jewish nation; but in their failing to practice the truth they are ignorant both of the Scriptures and the power of God. The power and influence of God's law are around about, but not within the soul, renewing it in true holiness; therefore the Lord sends His appeals to them to urge upon them the practice of what is right. The appeals of His Spirit are neglected and rejected. The barriers are broken down, and the soul is weak, and for want of moral force to overcome, is polluted and debased. They are binding themselves in bundles as fagots, ready to be consumed at the last day.

Duties and Obligations of Ministers. The Jewish priests were required to be, in person, all that was symmetrical and well-proportioned, that they might reflect a great truth. "Be ye clean that bear the vessels of the Lord." The Lord required not only a well-proportioned mind and symmetrical body of the Jews' ministry in holy office, but He required also pure and uncorrupted minds. And He requires no less of us, in this dispensation, in the ministry of the gospel. His called and chosen are to show forth the praises of Him who hath called them out of darkness into His marvelous light. The same Bible that contains the privileges of God's people, and His promises to them, contains also the sacred duties and the solemn obligations He requires of the shepherd who has charge of the flock of God; so that the people can see by comparing the living preacher with the divine picture whether he has credentials from heaven in likeness of character to Him who is the Chief Shepherd. God designs that the teacher of the Bible should in his character and home life be a specimen of the principles of the truth which he is teaching to his fellow men.

True Character an Inward Reflection. What a man is has greater influence than what he says. The quiet, consistent, godly life is a living epistle, known and read of all men. A man may speak and write like an angel, but his practices may resemble a fallen fiend. God will have the believers of the truth zealous to maintain good works. As they occupy high positions, they will be tested by a higher standard. They will be sifted; defects and vices will be searched out; for if such exist, they will be developed in words and deportment. True character is not something shaped from without, or put on, but it is something radiating from within. If true goodness, purity, meekness, lowliness, and equity are dwelling in the heart, that fact will be reflected in the character; and such a character is full of power.

Faults and Practices of a Few. The officers who were sent to take Jesus reported that ''never man spake like this Man.'' But the reason of this was that never man lived like this Man; for if He had not so lived, He could not so have spoken. His words bore with them a convincing power, because they came from a heart pure, holy, burdened with love and sympathy, beneficence and truth. How rejoiced are those who hate God's law, to find spot and stain of character in one who stands in defense of that law! They are only too glad to cast a reproach upon all the loyal and true, because of the faults and impure practices of a few.

There is eloquence in the quiet and consistent life of a pure, true, unadulterated Christian. We shall have temptations as long as we are in this world; but instead of injuring us, they will only be turned to our advantage, if resisted. The bounds are placed where Satan cannot pass. He may prepare the furnace that consumes the dross, but instead of injury, it can only bring forth the gold of the character, purer, upon higher vantage ground than before the trial.

At Baal-peor. The crime that brought the judgments of God upon Israel was that of licentiousness. The forwardness of women to entrap souls did not end at Baal-peor. Notwithstanding the punishment that followed the sinners in Israel, the same crime was repeated many times. Satan was most active in seeking to make Israel's overthrow complete. Balak by the advice of Balaam laid the snare. Israel would have bravely met their enemies in battle, and resisted them, and come off conquerors; but when women invited their attention and sought their company and beguiled them by their charms, they did not resist temptations. They were invited to idolatrous feasts, and their indulgence in wine further beclouded their dazed minds.

The power of self-control, their allegiance to God's law, was not preserved. Their senses were so beclouded with wine, and their unholy passions had such full sway, overpowering every barrier, that they invited temptation, even to the attending of these idolatrous feasts. Those who had never flinched in battle, who were brave men, did not barricade their souls to resist temptation to indulge their basest passions. Idolatry and licentiousness went together. They first defiled their conscience by lewdness, and then departed from God still further by idolatry, thus showing contempt for the God of Israel.

Satan's Repetitious Plots. Near the close of this earth's history Satan will work with all his powers in the same manner and with the same temptations wherewith he tempted ancient Israel just before their entering the land of promise. He will lay snares for those who claim to keep the commandments of God, and who are almost on the borders of the heavenly Canaan. He will use his powers to their utmost in order to entrap souls, and to take God's professed people upon their weakest points. Those who have not brought the lower passions into subjection to the higher powers of their being, those who have allowed their minds to flow in a channel of carnal indulgence of the baser passions, Satan is determined to destroy with his temptations— to pollute their souls with licentiousness.

He is not aiming especially at the lower and less important marks, but he makes use of his snares through those whom he can enlist as his agents to allure or attract men to take liberties which are condemned in the law of God. And men in responsible positions, teaching the claims of God's law, whose mouths are filled with arguments in vindication of His law, against which Satan has made such a raid—over such he sets his hellish powers and his agencies at work, and overthrows them upon the weak points in their character, knowing that he who offends on one point is guilty of all, thus obtaining complete mastery over the entire man.

Mind, soul, body, and conscience are involved in the ruin. If he be a messenger of righteousness, and has had great light, or if the Lord has used him as His special worker in the cause of truth, then how great is the triumph of Satan! How he exults! How God is dishonored!

Licentiousness, One of Satan's Enchantments. The licentious practice of the Hebrews accomplished for them that which all the warfare of nations and the enchantments of Balaam could not do. They became separated from their God. Their covering and protection were removed from them. God turned to be their enemy. So many of the princes and people were guilty of licentiousness, that it became a national sin; for God was wroth with the whole congregation.

The very same Satan is now working to the very same end, to weaken and destroy the people who claim to be keeping the commandments of God, as they are just on the borders of the heavenly Canaan. Satan knows it is his time. He has but little time left now in which to work, and he will work with tremendous power to ensnare the people of God upon their weak points of character.

Women as Tempters. There will be women who will become tempters, and who will do their best to attract and win the attention of men to themselves. First, they will seek to win their sympathy, next their affections, and then to induce them to break God's holy law. Those who have dishonored their minds and affections by placing them where God's Word forbids, will not scruple to dishonor God by various species of idolatry. God will leave them to their vile affections.

It is necessary to guard the thoughts; to fence the soul about with the injunctions of God's Word; and to be very careful in every thought, word, and action not to be betrayed into sin. It is necessary to guard against the cultivation of the indulgence of the lower passions. This is not the fruit of sanctified thoughts or hearts.

It is now the duty of God's commandment-keeping people to watch and pray, to search the Scriptures diligently, to hide the word of God in the heart, lest they sin against Him in idolatrous thoughts and debasing practices, and thus the church of God become demoralized like the fallen churches whom prophecy represents as being filled with every unclean and hateful bird.—RH May 17, 1887.

Fitted for Translation. There is to be a people fitted up for translation to heaven, whom Enoch represents. They are looking and waiting for the coming of the Lord. The work will go on with all those who will cooperate with Jesus in the work of redemption. He gave Himself for us that He might redeem us from all iniquity, and purify unto Himself a peculiar people, zealous of good works. God has made every provision that they should be intelligent Christians, filled with a knowledge of His will in all wisdom and spiritual understanding.

A theoretical knowledge of the truth is essential, but the knowledge of the greatest truth will not save us; our knowledge must be practical. God's people must not only know His will, but they must practice it. Many will be purged out from the numbers of those who know the truth, because they are not sanctified by it. The truth must be brought into their hearts, sanctifying and cleansing them from all earthliness and sensuality in the most private life. The soul temple must be cleansed. Every secret act is as if we were in the presence of God and holy angels, as all things are open before God, and from Him nothing can be hid.

Demoralizing Practices in Marriage. In this age of our world the marriage vows are often disregarded. God never designed that marriage should cover the multitude of sins that are practiced. Sensuality and base practices in a marriage relation are educating the mind and moral taste for demoralizing practices outside the marriage relation.

God is purifying a people to have clean hands and pure hearts to stand before Him in the judgment. The standard must be elevated, the imagination purified; the infatuation clustering around debasing practices must be given up, and the soul uplifted to pure thoughts, holy practices. All who will stand the test and trial just before us, will be partakers of the divine nature, having escaped, not participated in, the corruptions that are in the world through lust.

Source of Spiritual Power. The works of Satan are not half discerned, because purity and holiness do not mark the life and character of those who claim to be ministers of Christ. Strengthened with all might, according to His glorious power, we are thus fortified against the temptations of Satan. Christ and His purity and His matchless charms should be the soul's contemplation. There is spiritual power for all, which they may have if they will, that they may resist temptation, that duty may be done and the soul hold fast its integrity. Those who feel their need of being strengthened by might by God's Spirit in the inner man, will not lose their integrity. Earnest prayer and watching thereunto will carry them through temptations. We must be united to Christ by living faith.

Like Christ in Character. We are now amid the perils of the last days. Satan has come down with great power to work his deceptions. He fastens the mind or imaginations upon impure, unlawful things. Christians become like Christ in character by dwelling upon the divine Model. That with which they come in contact has a molding influence upon life and character.

I have read of a painter who would never look upon an imperfect painting for a single moment, lest it should have a deteriorating influence upon his own eye and conceptions. That which we allow ourselves to look upon oftenest, and think of most, transfers itself in a measure to us. The imagination trained to dwell upon God and His loveliness will not find delight in dwelling upon scenes that are created by the imagination that is excited by lust. . . .

The Infernal Wisdom of Satan. Satan is at work now as he worked in Eden, as he has worked through all successive generations. The archfiend knows well with what material he has to deal. He knows the weak points in every character; and if these weak points are not strengthened, he will display his infernal wisdom in his devices to overthrow the very strongest men, princes in the army of Israel. All along through successive generations are wrecks of character which have been destroyed because the soul was not garrisoned. And now as we near the close of time, Satan will work with masterly activity to undermine principle, and corrupt moral character.

Sin is committed by many who think their crime is effectually concealed. But there is One who says, "I know thy works"; "there is nothing covered which shall not be revealed; and hid, which shall not be known." When the mind is infatuated with the idea of sin, there will be deception practiced; lies will be told; for those who commit such sins will not be slow to lie as well. But all sin shall be revealed.

No Concealing of Sins From God. God sees the sinner. The eye which never slumbers knows everything that is done. It is written in His book. One may conceal his sin from father, mother, wife, and friends, and yet all lies open before God, and is placed in His book of record. . . . David was a repentant man, and although he confessed and hated his sin, he could not forget it.

He exclaimed, "Whither shall I go from Thy Spirit? or whither shall I flee from Thy presence? If I ascend up into heaven, Thou art there: if I make my bed in hell, behold, Thou art there. If I take the wings of the morning, and dwell in the uttermost parts of the sea; even there shall Thy hand lead me. . . . Yea, the darkness hideth not from Thee; but the night shineth as the day" [Ps. 139:7-12].

God is everywhere. He sees, He knows, all things, and understands the intents and purposes of the heart. It is in vain that an attempt should be made to conceal sin from His notice. He saw our first parents in Eden. He saw Cain when he raised his hand to kill Abel. He saw the sins of the inhabitants of the old world, and numbered their days and punished them with a flood. He saw the sins of His own covenant people, the Jews, when they plotted against the life of the Son of God.

Book of God's Remembrance. As surely does He mark every transgression, and every secret thing will be brought into judgment. They may be hid from mortal man, they may be hid from the good, the pure, and the holy, from friends and from foes; yet God sees them. All sins will be revealed in the day of judgment, and unless they have been repented of beforehand, they will receive punishment according to their magnitude; for a record of all the deeds of men is kept in the book of God's remembrance. All the good actions, all the evil actions, of life are recorded.

The fact that the accumulated sins are treasured up and at last exposed, is a terrible fact; and why those professing to be sons and daughters of God venture, in the face of light, in the face of knowledge, to sin against their own conscience and by their sin involve others in the same ruin, is a mystery. Have they ever tasted of the powers of the world to come? Have they ever enjoyed sweet communion with God? Then how can they turn to sensual, condemning, soul-degrading practices?

The Day of God's Revealings. The last great day is right upon us. Let all consider that Satan is now striving for the mastery over souls. He is playing the game of life for your souls. Will there be sins committed by you on the very borders of the heavenly Canaan? Oh, what revealings! The husband will know for the first time the deception and falsehood that have been practiced by the wife whom he thought innocent and pure. The wife for the first time will know the case of her husband, and the relatives and friends will see how error and falsehood and corruption have been clustering about them; for the secrets of all hearts will stand revealed. The hour of judgment is almost here—long delayed by the goodness and mercy of God. But the trump of God will sound, to the consternation of the unprepared who are living, and awaken the pale nations of the dead. The great white throne will appear, and all the righteous dead will come forth to immortality.

Whatever have been the little sins indulged [they] will

ruin the soul, unless they are overcome. The small sins will swell into the greater sins. Impure thoughts, private, impure actions, unrefined, low, and sensual thoughts and actions in the marriage life, the giving of loose reins to the baser passions under the marriage vow, will lead to every other sin, the transgression of all the commandments of God.

Tyrannical Growth of Human Weakness. Men that God has entrusted with noble talents will be, unless closely connected with God, guilty of great weakness, and, not having the grace of Christ in the soul, will become connected with greater crimes. This is because they do not make the truth of God a part of them. Their discipline has been defective; the soul culture has not been carried forward from one advance to another; inborn tendencies have not been restrained, but have degraded the soul. For all the natural weaknesses Jesus has made ample provision, that they may be overcome through His grace. If not overcome, the weakness will become a tyrant, a conqueror, to overcome them, and the heavenly light will become beclouded and extinguished.

Intellectual Greatness Insufficient. I feel compelled to write most earnestly on this point because I feel the peril that is upon us. We have in past history the example of most painful characters showing the danger of men in high places being corrupted. Men of masterly minds, who possessed large talents of influence, yet did not put their trust wholly in God, but allowed themselves to be praised and petted and lauded by the world's great men, lost their balance, and thought that great men's sins were not vices. The heavenly guide left them, and their course was rapidly downward to corruption and perdition. They completely lost the just standard of honor, lost all distinction between right and wrong, between sin and righteousness. There are lights and shades in character, and one or the other certainly triumphs.

But God in heaven is weighing moral worth. He will judge righteously. The wicked will not always remain unchecked. Nothing but grace and truth brought into the inner life, inwrought in the character, is sufficient to keep the greatest, the most talented, men morally erect. If intellectual greatness could have been sufficient, their characters would have been firm as a rock. But they needed virtuous characters. Paul says, I am what I am by the grace of God that is in me. God's people must arise, and gird themselves with the whole armor of righteousness.—RH May 24, 1887.

Reasons for Israel's Failure. Many of ancient Israel fell just in sight of the promised land. What was their sin? Licentiousness. And these unholy passions of the heart are controlling with masterly power many of those who claim to be following Christ. The words and works of many who know the truth are corrupt. They have reasoning power, they comprehend the truth, but have not been thoroughly converted; have not felt the saving power of the truth upon their souls. They do not entertain Christ as an honored guest in their house. Sensual gratification is corroding the entire man, tainting and corrupting the entire household. . . . The purity and sanctity of the marriage relation instituted in Eden to be kept sacred, elevated, is brought down to administer to lust.—Ms 31, 1885.

David's Departure From Right. God selected David, a humble shepherd, to rule His people. He was strict in all the ceremonies connected with the Jewish religion, and he distinguished himself by his boldness and unwavering trust in God. He was remarkable for his fidelity and reverence. His firmness, humility, love of justice, and decision of character, qualified him to carry out the high purposes of God, to instruct Israel in their devotions, and to rule them as a generous and wise monarch.

His religious character was sincere and fervent. It was while David was thus true to God, and possessing these exalted traits of character, that God called him a man after His own heart. When exalted to the throne, his general course was in striking contrast with the kings of other nations. He abhorred idolatry, and zealously kept the people of Israel from being seduced into idolatry by the surrounding nations. He was greatly beloved and honored by his people.

He often conquered, and triumphed. He increased in wealth and greatness. But his prosperity had an influence to lead him from God. His temptations were many and strong.

Sad Result of Polygamy. He finally fell into the common practice of other kings around him, of having a plurality of wives, and his life was embittered by the evil results of polygamy. His first wrong was in taking more than one wife, thus departing from God's wise arrangement. This departure from right prepared the way for greater errors. The kingly idolatrous nations considered it an addition to their honor and dignity to have many wives, and David regarded it an honor to his throne to possess several wives. But he was made to see the wretched evil of such a course by the unhappy discord, rivalry, and jealousy among his numerous wives and children.

David's Repentance. His crime in the case of Uriah and Bathsheba was heinous in the sight of God. A just and impartial God did not sanction or excuse these sins in David, but sends a reproof, and heavy denunciation by Nathan, His prophet, which portrays in living colors his grievous offense. David had been blinded to his wonderful departure from God. He had excused his own sinful course to himself until his ways seemed possible in his own eyes. One wrong step had prepared the way for another, until his sins called for the rebuke from Jehovah through Nathan.

David awakens as from a dream. He feels the sense of his sin. He does not seek to excuse his course, or palliate his sin, as did Saul; but with remorse and sincere grief, he bows his head before the prophet of God, and acknowledges his guilt. Nathan tells David that because of his repentance and humble confession, God will forgive his sin, and avert a part of the threatened calamity, and spare his life.

Transgression and Punishment. Yet he should be punished, because he had given great occasion to the enemies of the Lord to blaspheme. This occasion has been improved by the enemies of God, from David's day until the present time. Skeptics have assailed Christianity and ridiculed the Bible, because David gave them occasion. They bring up to Christians the case of David—his sin in the case of Uriah and Bathsheba, his polygamy—and then assert that David is called a man after God's own heart; and if the Bible record is correct, God justified David in his crimes.

I was shown that it was when David was pure, and walking in the counsel of God, that God called him a man after His own heart. When David departed from God, and stained his virtuous character by his crimes, he was no longer a man after God's own heart. God did not in the least degree justify him in his sins, but sent Nathan, His prophet, with dreadful denunciations to David because he had transgressed the commandment of the Lord.

God shows His displeasure at David's having a plurality of wives by visiting him with judgments, and permitting evils to rise up against him from his own house. The terrible calamity God permitted to come upon David, who for his integrity was once called a man after God's own heart, is evidence to after generations that God would not justify anyone in transgressing His commandments, but that He will surely punish the guilty, however righteous and favored of God they might once have been while they followed the Lord in purity of heart. When the righteous turn from their righteousness to do evil, their past righteousness will not save them from the wrath of a just and holy God.

Saints' Sins in the Bible. Leading men of Bible history have sinned grievously. Their sins are not concealed, but faithfully recorded in the history of God's church, with the punishment from God which followed the offenses. These instances are left on record for the benefit of after generations, and should inspire faith in the Word of God, as a faithful history. Men who wish to doubt God, doubt Christianity, and the Word of God, will not judge candidly, and impartially, but with prejudiced minds will scan the life and character to detect all the defects in the life of those who have been the most eminent leaders of Israel.

A faithful delineation of character, God has caused to be given in inspired history, of the best and greatest men in their day. These men were mortal, subject to a tempting devil. Their weakness and sins are not covered, but are faithfully recorded, with the reproof and punishment which followed. "These things were written for our admonition upon whom the ends of the world are come."

God has not allowed much said in His Word to extol the virtues of the best men that have lived upon the earth. All their victories and great and good works were ascribed to God. He alone was to receive the glory, He alone to be exalted. He was all and in all. Man was only an agent, a feeble instrument, in His hands. The power and excellence were all of God. God saw in man a continual disposition to depart from, and to forget Him, and worship the creature instead of the Creator. Therefore God would not suffer much in the praise of man to be left upon the pages of sacred history.

The Penitential Psalms. David repented of his sin, in dust and ashes. He entreated the forgiveness of God, and concealed not his repentance from the great men, and even servants of His kingdom. He composed a penitential psalm, recounting his sin and repentance, which psalm he knew would be sung by after generations. He wished others to be instructed by the sad history of his life.

The songs which David composed were sung by all Israel, especially in the presence of the assembled court, and before priests, elders, and lords. He knew that the confession of his guilt would bring his sins to the notice of other generations. He presents his case, showing in whom was his trust and hope for pardon. "Have mercy upon me, O God, according to Thy lovingkindness; according unto the multitude of Thy tender mercies blot out my transgressions. Wash me throughly from mine iniquity, and cleanse me from my sin." "Deliver me from bloodguiltiness, O God, Thou God of my salvation" [Ps. 51:1, 2, 14].

David does not manifest the spirit of an unconverted man. If he had possessed the spirit of the rulers of the nations around him, he would not have borne from Nathan the picture of his crime before him in its truly abominable colors, but would have taken the life of the faithful reprover. But notwithstanding the loftiness of his throne, and his unlimited power, his humble acknowledgment of all with which he was charged is evidence that he still feared and trembled at the word of the Lord.

Results of David's Wrongdoing. David was made to feel bitterly the fruits of wrongdoing. His sons acted over the sins of which he had been guilty. Amnon committed a great crime. Absalom revenged it by slaying him. Thus was

David's sin brought continually to his mind, and he was made to feel the full weight of the injustice done to Uriah and Bathsheba.—4SGa 85-89.

Warnings in Others' Examples. God's reproof has been plainly uttered against men and women who have sinned by corrupting their bodies and defiling their souls by licentiousness. They have the warnings to others placed in similar circumstances, who have been overcome by the tempter, and they know that the displeasure of God rested upon them. . . . God has expressed condemnation of sin in all its forms. The sin of licentiousness is plainly rebuked and condemned. Men and women will be judged according to the light given them of God.—TM 437.

Control by Sanctified Reason. Every unholy passion must be kept under the control of sanctified reason, through the grace abundantly bestowed of God in every emergency. But let no arrangement be made to create an emergency; let there be no voluntary act to place one where he will be assailed with temptation or give the least occasion for others to think him guilty of indiscretion.—1MCP 237.

Correct View of Self in Light of God's Word. Satan's constant temptations are designed to weaken man's government over his own heart, to undermine his power of self-control. He leads man to break the bands which connect him in holy, happy union with his Maker. Then when he is disconnected from God, passion obtains control over reason, and impulse over principle, and he becomes sinful in thought and action; his judgment is perverted, his reason seems to be enfeebled, and he needs to be restored to himself by being restored to God by a correct view of himself in the light of God's Word.—1MCP 228.

The Power of Religion. By what means shall the young man repress his evil propensities, and develop what is noble and good in his character? The will, intellect, and emotions when controlled by the power of religion will become transformed. "Whether therefore ye eat or drink, or whatsoever ye do, do all to the glory of God" [1 Cor. 10:31]. Here is a principle underlying every act, thought, and motive if the entire being is under control of the will of God.

The voice and passions must be crucified. "I can do all things through Christ which strengtheneth me" [Phil. 4:13]. The will, the appetites and passions, will clamor for indulgence, but God has implanted within you desires for high and holy purposes; and it is not necessary that these should be debased. This is so only when we refuse to submit to the control of reason and conscience. We are to restrain our passions and deny self.

Satan's Pursuit of the Youth. The unsanctified mind fails to receive the strength and comfort which God has provided for all who will come to Him. There is an unrest, a burning desire for something new, to gratify, to please and fascinate the mind, and this indulgence is called pleasure. Satan has alluring charms with which to engage the interest and excite the imagination of youth, and fasten them in his snare. Do not build your character on the sand.—Ms 59, 1900.

12. Disregard of the Seventh Commandment

God's Law the Way to Happiness. Previous to the destruction of the old world by a flood, its inhabitants were reeking in corruption. Sin and crime of every description prevailed. The state of the world now is fast reaching the point when God will say to it, as He did anciently: "My Spirit shall not always strive with man." One of the grievous sins existing in this degenerate age of corruption is adultery. This shameful sin is practiced to an alarming extent. The Sabbath and the marriage institution were ordained of God in Eden to be preserved sacred and holy. Both of these institutions of divine appointment have been disregarded and set at naught by men and women whose hearts are fully set in them to do evil.

Adultery a "Christian" Sin. But if the transgressors of the seventh commandment were to be found only among those who do not profess to be Christ's followers, the evil would not be a tenth part as great as it now is; but the crime of adultery is largely committed by professed Christians. Both clergymen and laymen, whose names stand fair upon the church record, are alike guilty.

Many who profess to be the ministers of Christ are like the sons of Eli who ministered in the sacred office and took advantage of their office to engage in crime and commit adultery, causing the people to transgress the law of God. A fearful account will such have to render when the cases of all shall pass in review before God, and they be judged according to the deeds done in the body. . . . Adultery is one of the terrible sins of this age. This sin exists among professed Christians of every class. . . .

Christians are called to lay their bodies a living sacrifice upon the altar of God. "Let not sin therefore reign in your mortal body, that ye should obey it in the lusts thereof. Neither yield ye your members as instruments of unrighteousness unto sin; but yield yourselves unto God, as those that are alive from the dead, and your members as instruments of righteousness unto God" [Rom. 6:12, 13].

If the bodies professedly laid upon the altar of God should pass that scrutiny that was given the Jewish sacrifice, how few would stand the test and be pronounced perfect before God, preserved unto holiness, free from the taints of sin or pollution. No lame sacrifice could God receive. No injured or diseased sacrifice would God accept. The offering given to God was required to be sound, in every respect without blemish, and valuable.

Origin of Impure Acts. None can glorify God in their body, as He requires, while they are living in transgression of the law of God. If the body violates the seventh commandment, it is through the dictation of the mind. If the mind is impure, the body will naturally engage in impure acts. Purity cannot exist in the soul of one who yields his body to impure acts. If the body is serving lust, the mind cannot maintain consecration to God. To preserve a sanctified mind, the body must be preserved in sanctification and honor. The mind will then serve the law of God, and yield willing obedience to all its claims. Then, with the apostle, such can yield their members as instruments of righteousness unto God. . . .

No Real Enjoyment of Life for Sinners. The Lord made man upright; but he has fallen, and become degraded, because he refuses to yield obedience to the sacred claims which the law of God has upon him. All the passions of man, if properly controlled and rightly directed, will contribute to his physical and moral health, and insure to him a great amount of happiness. The adulterer, the fornicator, and the incontinent, do not enjoy life. There can be no true enjoyment for the transgressor of God's law. The Lord knew this, therefore He restricts man. He directs, commands, and He positively forbids. . . . The Lord well knew that the happiness of His children depends upon their submission to His authority, and living in obedience to this holy, just, and good rule of government.

Thoughts and Actions Open to God. Man may pass on awhile, and conceal the fact that he is an adulterer; yet God has His eye upon him. He marks the man. He cannot conceal his crimes from God. He may apparently conduct himself properly before his family and before the community, and be esteemed a good man. But does he deceive himself in thinking there is not knowledge with the Most High?

He is exposing his corruption to the view of the Majesty of Heaven. He who is high and lifted up, and the train of whose glory fills the temple, sees and knows even the thoughts and the intents and purposes of the heart of the transgressor who is debasing himself in the sight of the pure, sinless angels, who are recording all the acts of the children of men. And not only is his sin seen, but it is marked by the recording angel.

The transgressor of God's law may pass on for a time without exposure; but, sooner or later, he will find himself overtaken, exposed, and condemned. Whoever dares to violate the law of God will experience for himself that "the way of the transgressor is hard."—RH March 8, 1870.

God's All-Seeing Eye. If we were to cherish an habitual impression that God sees and hears all that we do and say and keeps a faithful record of our words and actions, and that we must meet it all, we would fear to sin. Let the young ever remember that wherever they are, and whatever they do, they are in the presence of God. No part of our conduct escapes observation. We cannot hide our ways from the Most High.

Human laws, though sometimes severe, are often transgressed without detection, and hence with impunity; but not so with the law of God. The deepest midnight is no cover for the guilty one. He may think himself alone, but to every deed there is an unseen witness. The very motives of his heart are open to divine inspection. Every act, every word, every thought, is as distinctly marked as though there were only one person in the whole world, and the attention of heaven were centered upon him.—PP 217, 218.

Professed Commandment-keepers Guilty. Even some who profess to keep all the commandments of God are guilty of the sin of adultery. What can I say to arouse their benumbed sensibilities? Moral principle, strictly carried out, becomes the only safeguard of the soul.—2T 352.

The Greater the Knowledge, the Greater the Sin. Not all who profess to keep the commandments of God possess their bodies in sanctification and honor. The most solemn message ever committed to mortals has been entrusted to this people, and they can have a powerful influence if they will be sanctified by it. They profess to be standing upon the elevated platform of eternal truth, keeping all of God's commandments; therefore, if they indulge in sin, if they commit fornication and adultery, their crime is of tenfold greater magnitude than is that of the classes I have named [First-day Adventists], who do not acknowledge the law of God as binding upon them. In a peculiar sense do those who profess to keep God's law dishonor Him and reproach the truth by transgressing its precepts.

The Sad Example of Israel. It was the prevalence of this very sin, fornication, among ancient Israel, which brought upon them the signal manifestation of God's displeasure. His judgments then followed close upon their heinous sin; thousands fell, and their polluted bodies were left in the wilderness. . . .

"Now all these things happened unto them for ensamples: and they are written for our admonition, upon whom the ends of the world are come. Wherefore let him that thinketh he standeth take heed lest he fall'' [1 Cor. 10: 11, 12]. Seventh-day Adventists, above all other people in the world, should be patterns of piety, holy in heart and in conversation.—2T 450, 451.

13. Dealing With Impure Thoughts and Suggestions

Need for Clear Spiritual Eyesight. Never was there a time when Christian men and women, in all walks of life, were in so great need of clear spiritual eyesight as now. It is not safe to lose sight of Christ for one moment. His followers must pray, and believe, and love Him fervently.

A very thorough work must be done in cleansing the soul temple from its natural depravity. The Christian must be wide awake to resist the increeping of a spirit of licentiousness among those who claim to be sanctified. When our hearts are clean, washed, and made white by the blood of the Lamb, the work will go forward in our experience that was outlined in the wonderful prayer of Christ: ''For their sakes I sanctify Myself, that they also might be sanctified through the truth'' [John 17:19].

What shall be said regarding the man who has been greatly blessed as a teacher of righteousness, yet who in time of temptation is betrayed into a sinful course? Satan in the form of a heavenly angel has come to him as he approached Christ in the wilderness of temptation, and he has gained the victory. . . .

Satan's Disguise as an Angel of Light. It is those who have had the most light that Satan most assiduously seeks to ensnare. He knows that if he can deceive them, they will, under his control, clothe sin with garments of righteousness, and lead many astray. I say to all, Be on your guard; for as an angel of light, Satan is walking in every assembly of Christian workers, and in every church, trying to win the members to his side. I am bidden to give to the people of God the warning, "Be not deceived: God is not mocked."—RH May 14, 1908.

The Curse of Transgression. Oh, that men and women would consider and inquire what is to be gained by transgressing God's law! At all times and in all places, under any and every circumstance, transgression is a terrible mistake, a dishonor to God and a curse to man. We must regard it thus, however fair its guise and by whomsoever it is committed. As Christ's ambassador I entreat of you who profess present truth to promptly resent any approach to impurity, and forsake the society of those who intimate or breathe an impure suggestion. Loathe these defiling sins with the most intense hatred. Fly from those who would even in conversation let their minds run in such a channel, "for out of the abundance of the heart the mouth speaketh." Shun them as you would the leprosy.

I call upon all who have had any confidence in these pretenders whose lives are not elevated and whose conversation is not pure, to measure them by the gospel rule: "To the law and to the testimony; if they speak not according to this word, it is because there is no light in them" (Isa. 8:20). Let the mirror of God's Word reflect upon them, and discern the defects in their moral character.

Offensive Character of Sin. We are in an age of the world when there is a fascinating, mesmeric power in all that class who would gloss over sin, secretly insinuating impure thoughts and coming as angels of light while they are the servants of sin. They do not sense the offensive character of sin or the retributive justice of God that will fall upon the sinner. I tremble for those who are not fully upon their guard, and who will be in danger of being deceived and corrupted. As a servant of Jesus Christ I warn you to shun the company of this class. Let them not into your houses, neither bid them Godspeed. Separate yourselves from their company, for they corrupt the very atmosphere you breathe. . . .

As Moses called to Israel that they leave the tents of Korah, Dathan, and Abiram, we would call for all to leave these corrupt men alone to suffer the disgrace and punishment of their crimes.

Satan in the Form of a Man. As God has shown me how abhorrent in His sight are these defiling sins, and as they are steadily increasing in our world and would intrude into our churches, I warn you to give no place to the devil. Fly from the seducer. Though a minister, he is Satan in the form of a man. He has borrowed the livery of heaven that he may serve his master and deceive souls. You should not for one moment give place to an impure, covert suggestion. Grant no indulgence. Rebuke them. Associate not with them, no not so much as to eat [with them]. Regard with no complaisance the words that would tarnish your soul's purity. Even listening to an impure suggestion will stain the soul, as foul, impure water will defile the channel through which it passes.

Clear as the Light of the Sun. Choose poverty, separation from friends, losses, reproaches, or any suffering, rather than to defile the soul with sin. Death before dishonor or the transgression of God's law, should be the motto of every Christian. As a people professing to be reformers, treasuring the most sacred, solemn, purifying truths of God's Word, we must elevate the standard far higher than it is at the present time. Sin and sinners in the church must be promptly dealt with, that others may fear God. Truth and purity require that we make more thorough work to cleanse the camp of the Achans.

Let those in responsible positions not suffer sin in a

brother. Show him that he must either put away his sins or be separated from the church. When the individual members of the church shall act as true followers of the meek and lowly Saviour, there will be less covering up and excusing of sin. All will strive to act at all times as if in God's presence. They will realize that the eye of God is ever upon them and that the most secret thought is known to Him. The character, the motives, the desires and purposes, are as clear as the light of the sun to the eye of the Omniscient.

Peril of Indulged Sin. By far the larger class do not bear this in mind because they do not cultivate spirituality and test their character by God's standard of right. They do not bear constantly in mind that a fearful account must be rendered at the bar of God by all the transgressors of His law. The life must be ordered and fashioned as in the eye of the great Taskmaster. Can you who have professed to receive such great light in advance of every other people on the face of the earth, be content with a low level?

Oh, how earnestly and constantly should we seek for the Divine Presence, that there may be not only a profession but a realization of the solemn truth that the end of all things is at hand and that the Judge of all the earth standeth at the door! How can you disregard His just and holy requirements? How can you transgress in the very face of Jehovah? Can you pursue a course of sin in full view of the consequences? Can you cherish unholy thoughts and base passions in the full view of the pure angels and of the Redeemer, who gave Himself for you that He might redeem you from all iniquity, and purify unto Himself a peculiar people, zealous of good works? Can we be guiltless and cherish sin in the sight of God? As you contemplate the matter in the light which shines from the cross of Christ, will not sin appear too mean, too perilous, too fearful, to indulge in?

Spotless and Undefiled Until the End. Sinful corruptions! How sinful at any time, but how much more so now, when standing upon the very borders of the eternal world! I speak to my people. If you draw close to Jesus and seek to adorn your profession by a well-ordered life and godly conversation, your feet will be kept from straying into forbidden paths. If you will only watch, continually watch, unto prayer; if you will do everything as if you were in the immediate presence of God, you will be saved from yielding to temptation and may hope to be kept pure, spotless, and undefiled unto the end.

If you hold the beginning of your confidence firm unto the end, all your way will be established in God, and what grace has begun glory shall crown in the kingdom of our God. "The fruit of the Spirit is love, joy, peace, longsuffering, gentleness, goodness, faith, meekness, temperance: against such there is no law" [Gal. 5:22, 23]. If Christ be within us, we shall crucify the flesh with the affections and lusts.—Ms 9, 1880.

Purification of the Heart. By accepting Christ as his personal Saviour, man is brought into the same close relation to God, and enjoys His special favor, as does His own beloved Son. He is honored and glorified and intimately associated with God, his life being hid with Christ in God. Oh, what love, what wondrous love!

This is my teaching of moral purity. The opening of the blackness of impurity will not be one half as efficacious in uprooting sin as will the presentation of these grand and ennobling themes. The Lord has not given to women a message to assail men and charge them with their impurity and incontinence. They create sensuality in place of uprooting it. The Bible, and the Bible alone, has given the true lessons upon purity. Then preach the Word.

Christ, the Propitiation for Sin. Such is the grace of God, such the love wherewith He hath loved us, even when we were dead in trespasses and sins, enemies in our minds by wicked works, serving divers lusts and pleasures, the slaves of debased appetites and passion, servants of sin and Satan. What depth of love is manifested in Christ, as He becomes the propitiation for our sins. Through the ministration of the Holy Spirit souls are led to find forgiveness of sins.

The purity, the holiness, of the life of Jesus as presented from the Word of God, possess more power to reform and transform the character than do all the efforts put forth in picturing the sins and crimes of men and the sure results. One steadfast look to the Saviour uplifted upon the cross will do more to purify the mind and heart from every defilement than will all the scientific explanations by the ablest tongue.

Forgiveness at the Cross. Before the cross the sinner sees his unlikeness of character to Christ. He sees the terrible consequences of transgression; he hates the sin that he has practiced, and he lays hold upon Jesus by living faith. He has judged his position of uncleanness in the light of the presence of God and the heavenly intelligences. He has measured it by the standard of the cross. He has weighed it in the balances of the sanctuary. The purity of Christ has revealed to him his own impurity in its odious colors. He turns from the defiling sin; he looks to Jesus, and lives.

He finds an all-absorbing, commanding, attractive character in Jesus Christ, the One who died to deliver him from the deformity of sin, and with quivering lip and tearful eye he declares, "He shall not have died for me in vain."— Letter 102, 1894.

OTHER SEXUAL EVILS

14. Sexual Excess Within Marriage

Celibacy in Married State Not Recommended. My dear brother: I wish to present before you some things concerning the dangers that threaten the work at the present time. The work of Anna Phillips does not bear the signature of heaven.* I know what I am talking about. In our first experience in the infancy of this cause we had to meet similar manifestations. Many such revelations were given, and we had a most disagreeable work in meeting this element and giving it no place. Some things stated in these revelations were fulfilled, and this led some to accept them as genuine.

Young, unmarried women, would have a message for married men, and in no delicate words would tell them to their face of the abuse of the marriage privileges. Purity was the burden of the messages given, and for a while everything appeared to be reaching a high state of purity and holiness. But the inwardness of these matters was opened to me. I was shown what would be the outcome of this teaching.

---

*In a "testimony" written on August 10, 1892, Anna Rice Phillips stated, "The time has come of which Paul spoke when he said, 'But this I say, brethren, the time is short: it remaineth, that both they that have wives be as though they had none.' . . . Satan will make you feel that you cannot give up this one thing, that it is yours by right my brother, but is it when God has spoken?"— White Estate Document File No. 363.

Those who were engaged in this work were not a superficial, immoral class, but persons who had been the most devoted workers. Satan saw an opportunity to take advantage of the state of things, and to disgrace the cause of God. Those who thought themselves able to bear any test without exciting their carnal propensities, were overcome, and several unmarried men and women were compelled to be married. I am afraid of those who feel so great a burden to labor in this direction. Satan works upon the imagination, so that impurity is the result, instead of purity.—Letter 103, 1894.

Jesus did not enforce celibacy upon any class of men. He came not to destroy the sacred relationship of marriage, but to exalt it and restore it to its original sanctity. He looks with pleasure upon the family relationship where sacred and unselfish love bears sway.—AH 121.

The Expenditure of Vital Energy. Many parents do not obtain the knowledge that they should in the married life. They are not guarded lest Satan take advantage of them and control their minds and their lives. They do not see that God requires them to control their married lives from all excesses. But very few feel it to be a religious duty to govern their passions. They have united themselves in marriage to the object of their choice, and therefore reason that marriage sanctifies the indulgence of the baser passions. Even men and women professing godliness give loose rein to their lustful passions, and have no thought that God holds them accountable for the expenditure of vital energy, which weakens their hold on life and enervates the entire system.

Excessive Sexual Indulgence. The marriage covenant covers sins of the darkest hue. Men and women professing godliness debase their own bodies through the indulgence of the corrupt passions, and thus lower themselves beneath the brute creation. They abuse the powers that God has given them to be preserved in sanctification and honor. Health and life are sacrificed upon the altar of base passion. The higher, nobler powers are brought into subjection to the animal propensities. Those who thus sin are not acquainted with the result of their course.

Could all see the amount of suffering that they bring upon themselves by their own sinful indulgence, they would be alarmed; and some, at least, would shun the course of sin that brings such dreaded wages. So miserable an existence is entailed upon a large class that death would be preferable to life; and many do die prematurely, their lives sacrificed in the inglorious work of excessive indulgence of the animal passions. Yet because they are married, they think they commit no sin.

Men and women, you will one day learn what is lust, and the result of its gratification. Passion of just as base a quality may be found in the marriage relation as outside of it.—RH Sept. 19, 1899.

The Wife's Dignity and Self-Respect. Many professed Christians who passed before me seemed destitute of moral restraint. They were more animal than divine. In fact, they were about all animal. Men of this type degrade the wife whom they have promised to nourish and cherish. She is made an instrument to minister to the gratification of low, lustful propensities. And very many women submit to become slaves to lustful passion; they do not possess their bodies in sanctification and honor. The wife does not retain the dignity and self-respect which she possessed previous to marriage.

This holy institution should have preserved and increased her womanly respect and holy dignity; but her chaste, dignified, godlike womanhood has been consumed upon the altar of base passion; it has been sacrificed to please her husband. She soon loses respect for the husband, who does not regard the laws to which the brute creation yield obedience. The married life becomes a galling yoke; for love dies out, and frequently distrust, jealousy, and hate take its place.

Mistrust Between Husband and Wife. No man can truly love his wife when she will patiently submit to become his slave, and minister to his depraved passions. In her passive submission, she loses the value she once possessed in his eyes. He sees her dragged down from everything elevating, to a low level; and soon he suspects that she will as tamely submit to be degraded by another as by himself. He doubts her constancy and purity, tires of her, and seeks new objects to arouse and intensify his hellish passions. The law of God is not regarded. . . .

The wife also becomes jealous of the husband, and suspects that if opportunity should offer, he would just as readily pay his addresses to another as to her. She sees that he is not controlled by conscience or the fear of God; all these sanctified barriers are broken down by lustful passions; all that is godlike in the husband is made the servant of low, brutish lust. . . .

Destructive Nature of Sexual Excess. When the wife yields her body and mind to the control of her husband, being passive to his will in all things, sacrificing her conscience, her dignity, and even her identity, she loses the opportunity of exerting that mighty influence for good which she should possess, to elevate her husband. She could soften his stern nature, and her sanctifying influence could be exerted in a manner to refine and purify, leading him to strive earnestly to govern his passions, and be more spiritually minded, that they might be partakers together of the divine nature, having escaped the corruption that is in the world through lust.

The power of influence can be great to lead the mind to high and noble themes, above the low, sensual indulgences for which the heart unrenewed by grace naturally seeks. If the wife feels that in order to please her husband she must come down to his standard, when animal passion is the principal basis of his love, and controls his actions, she displeases God; for she fails to exert a sanctifying influence upon her husband. If she feels that she must submit to his animal passions without a word of remonstrance, she does not understand her duty to him nor to her God. Sexual excess will effectually destroy a love for devotional exercises, will take from the brain the substance needed to nourish the system, and will most effectually exhaust the vitality. No woman should aid her husband in this work of self-destruction. She will not do it if she is enlightened, and has true love for him. . . .

Preservation of Mind and Body. Let God-fearing men and women awake to their duty. Many professed Christians are suffering with paralysis of nerve and brain because of their intemperance in this direction. Rottenness is in the bones and marrow of many who are regarded as good men, who pray and weep and who stand in high places, but whose polluted carcasses will never pass the portals of the heavenly city.

Oh, that I could make all understand their obligation to God to preserve the mental and physical organism in the best condition to render perfect service to their Maker. . . .

Transmission of Vice From Parents to Children. From their youth up they have weakened the brain and sapped the constitution by the gratification of animal passions. Self-denial and temperance should be the watchword in their married life; then the children born to them will not be so liable to have the moral and intellectual organs weak, and the animal strong. Vice in children is almost universal. Is there not a cause? Who have given them the stamp of character? May the Lord open the eyes of all to see that they are standing in slippery places!

From the picture that has been presented before me of the corruption of men and women professing godliness, I have feared that I should altogether lose confidence in humanity. I have seen that a fearful stupor is upon nearly all. It is almost impossible to arouse the very ones who should be awakened, so as to have any just sense of the power which Satan holds over minds. They are not aware of the corruption teeming all around them. Satan has blinded their minds, and lulled them to carnal security.

The failures in our efforts to bring others up to understand the great dangers that beset souls, have sometimes led me to fear that my ideas of the depravity of the human heart were exaggerated. But when facts are brought to us showing the sad deformity of one who has dared to minister in sacred things while corrupt at heart, one whose sin-stained hands have profaned the vessels of the Lord, I am sure that I have not drawn the picture any too strong.—RH Sept. 26, 1899.*

Abuse of Sexual Privileges. Let the husband and wife in their married life prove a help and a blessing to one

---

*The two *Review and Herald* articles of September 19 and 26, carried the general title, "Christianity in the Marriage Relation."

another. Let them consider the cost of every indulgence in intemperance and sensualism. These indulgences do not increase love, nor ennoble and elevate. Those who will indulge the animal passions and gratify lust will surely stamp upon their offspring the debasing practices, the grossness of their own physical and moral defilement.— Ms 3, 1897.

It is carrying that which is lawful to excess that makes it a grievous sin.—4T 505.

Those professing to be Christians . . . should duly consider the result of every privilege of the marriage relation, and sanctified principle should be the basis of every action.—2T 380.

Vital Importance of a Good Example. The animal passions, cherished and indulged, become very strong in this age, and untold evils in the marriage life are the sure results. In the place of the mind being developed and having the controlling power, the animal propensities rule over the higher and nobler powers until they are brought into subjection to the animal propensities. What is the result? Women's delicate organs are worn out and become diseased; childbearing is no more safe; sexual privileges are abused. Men are corrupting their own bodies; and the wife has become a bedservant to their inordinate, base lusts, until there is no fear of God before their eyes. . . .

Nothing but the truth of God can either make man savingly wise or keep him so. If there is an immortal life to be obtained, if a pure and holy character must be developed in order to gain entrance to the presence of the Lord God and the society of heavenly angels, then why do not teachers, physicians, and preachers act this in their example by their teaching? Why are they not more zealous for the Master? Why do they not have burning love for souls for whom Christ died?

If man is to become immortal, his mind must be in harmony with God's mind. The true disciple in the school of Christ, whose mind is in harmony with the mind of God, will be not only constantly learning, but teaching as well as learning, constantly reflecting light, teaching upward and away from the common, prevailing errors of this perverse and adulterous generation. . . .

A Christian is to be constantly watching the Pattern, and imitating the holy example of Jesus. Then a right spirit will be infused into the life and character of others. If God were daily sought in earnest, humble prayer for light and for guidance, there would be a sure detecting in the individual course of action; unholy practices and many unholy plans would be repressed, and Jesus would be made the rule of life.—Ms 14, 1888.

Lower Passions and an Unhealthy Mind. The lower passions are to be strictly guarded. The perceptive faculties are abused, terribly abused, when the passions are allowed to run riot. When the passions are indulged, the blood, instead of circulating to all parts of the body, thereby relieving the heart and clearing the mind, is called in undue amount to the internal organs. Disease comes as the result. The mind cannot be healthy until the evil is seen and remedied.—Ms 24, 1900.

Indulgence Weakens the Moral Powers. Said Paul, "With my mind serve I the law of God." Becloud this mind through indulgence of animal appetite and passions, and the moral powers are weakened, so that the sacred and common are placed upon a level.—1MCP 229.

15. Petting and Premarital Sex

Infatuation Not Love. You have spent hours of the night in her company because you were both infatuated. She professes love for you but she knows not the pure love of an unpretending heart. Satan has ensnared your soul. I was shown you fascinated, deceived, and Satan exults that one who has scarcely a trait of character that would make a happy wife and a happy home should have an influence to separate you from the mother who loves you with a change-less affection. In the name of the Lord, cease your attention to Mattie F or marry her—do not scandalize the cause of God. . . .

The intimacy formed with Mattie has not had a tendency to bring you nearer the Lord or to sanctify you through the truth. . . .

Mattie expects to consummate a marriage with you and you have given her encouragement to expect this by your attentions. But will you choose this piece of perversity as your wife, and will you separate your affections from your mother and the people of God? . . .

Better to Marry than to Continue Improper Attentions. If you persist in the course you have pursued it would be much better for you to marry her, for your course is as directly contrary to God's will as to marry her. Satan accomplishes his purpose all the same. If the atmosphere surrounding her is the most agreeable to you, if she meets your standard for a wife to stand at the head of your family; if, in your calm judgment, taken in the light given you of God, her example would be worthy of imitation, you might as well marry her as to be in her society and conduct yourselves as only man and wife should conduct themselves toward each other. You have about ruined yourself as it is. If through the period of your life you wish to enjoy the society of Mattie as you now appear to enjoy it and be fascinated with it, why not go a step farther than you already have and make yourself her lawful protector and have an undisputed right to devote the hours you choose in her company and be charmed with her presence night after night?

Your acts and conversation are offensive to God. The angels of God bear record of your words and your actions. The light has been given you but you have not heeded it. The course you have pursued is a reproach to the cause of God. Your behavior is unbecoming and unchristian. When you should both be in your beds you have been in one another's society and in one another's arms nearly the entire night. . . . You give occasion to our enemies to judge our people as being loose in morals.— Letter 3, 1879.

Violation of the Seventh Commandment. You were shown me in her [Mattie's] society hours of the night; you know best in what manner these hours were spent. You called on me to speak whether you had broken God's commandments. I ask you, Have you not broken them? How was your time employed hours together night after night? Were your position, your attitude, your affections such that you would want them all registered in the ledger of heaven? I saw, I heard, things that would make angels blush. . . . No young man should do as you have done to Mattie unless married to her; and I was much surprised to see that you did not sense this matter more keenly. . . .

Will you now change entirely, cut the last connection with Mattie? Will she do this on her part? If neither of you will do this, marry her at once and disgrace yourselves and the cause of God no more.—Letter 61, 1880.

16. Homosexuality*

Sodomitish Impurity. Oh, how disgusted is God with the tame, lifeless, Christless efforts made by some of those who profess to be His servants! God's work must be carried forward strongly and upward. This cannot be done unless the sensuality that corrupts the whole man is separated from the religious experience. This work must be done.

Church members need to fast and pray, striving earnestly to overcome by the blood of the Lamb and the word of their testimony. Not one particle of Sodomitish impurity will escape the wrath of God at the execution of the judgment. Those who do not repent of and forsake all uncleanness will fall with the wicked. Those who become members of the royal family and form God's kingdom in the earth made new, will be saints, not sinners. Isaiah 30:1-3, 8-16.

Those who have had great light and have disregarded it stand in a worse position than those who have not been given so many advantages. They exalt themselves, but not the Lord. The punishment inflicted on human beings will in every case be proportionate to the dishonor they have

---

*The 1977 Annual Council of the Seventh-day Adventist Church voted that "gross sexual perversions, including homosexual practices, are recognized as a misuse of sexual powers and a violation of the divine intention in marriage. As such they are just cause for divorce."—*General Actions,* p. 10. Reasons for which a person may be disfellowshipped from the Seventh-day Adventist Church include "homosexual practice and other perversions."—*Seventh-day Adventist Church Manual* (Revised 1986), p. 162.

brought on God. Many, by a course of self-indulgence, have put Christ to open shame.—Letter 159, 1901.

Basest Passions of the Human Heart. Indulgence in unlawful things has become a power to deprave mankind, to dwarf the mind and to pervert the faculties. Just such a state of things as exists today existed before the flood and before the destruction of Sodom. Dissipation is on the increase in our world. Handbills on which indecent pictures are printed are posted up along our streets to allure the eyes and deprave the morals. These presentations are of such a character as to stir up the basest passions of the human heart through corrupt imaginings. These corrupt imaginings are followed by defiling practices like those in which the Sodomites indulged. But the most terrible part of the evil is that it is practiced under the garb of sanctity. Our youth will be defiled, their thoughts degraded, and their souls polluted unless they are barricaded with the truth.—Letter 1, 1875.

Sodom's Sins Today. We are not ignorant of the fall of Sodom because of the corruption of its inhabitants. The prophet has here [Eze. 16:49] specified the particular evils which led to dissolute morals. We see the very sins now existing in the world which were in Sodom and which brought upon her the wrath of God, even to her utter destruction.—4BC 1161.

Strange Abandonment of Principle. Is there not enough transpiring about us to show us the dangers that beset our path? Everywhere are seen wrecks of humanity, broken-down family altars, broken-up families. There is a strange abandonment of principle, the standard of morality is lowered, and the earth is fast becoming a Sodom. The

Sodomitish practices which brought the judgment of God upon the world, and caused it to be deluged with water, and which caused Sodom to be destroyed by fire, are fast increasing. We are nearing the end. God has borne long with the perversity of mankind, but their punishment is no less certain. Let those who profess to be the light of the world, depart from all iniquity.—RH Nov. 10, 1884.

Impurity is today widespread, even among the professed followers of Christ. Passion is unrestrained; the animal propensities are gaining strength by indulgence, while the moral powers are constantly becoming weaker. . . . The sins that destroyed the antediluvians and the cities of the plain exist today—not merely in heathen lands, not only among popular professors of Christianity, but with some who profess to be looking for the coming of the Son of man. If God should present these sins before you as they appear in His sight, you would be filled with shame and terror.—5T 218.

17. Masturbation

High Resolve and Spiritual Life Destroyed. Secret vice is the destroyer of high resolve, earnest endeavor, and strength of will to form a good religious character. All who have any true sense of what is embraced in being a Christian know that the followers of Christ are under obligation as His disciples to bring all their passions, their physical powers and mental faculties into perfect subordination to His will. Those who are controlled by their passions cannot be followers of Christ. They are too much devoted to the service of their master, the originator of every evil, to leave their corrupt habits and choose the service of Christ.—CG 445, 446.

Vital Energy Is Depleted. The practice of secret habits surely destroys the vital forces of the system. All unnecessary vital action will be followed by corresponding depression. Among the young the vital capital, the brain, is so severely taxed at an early age that there is a deficiency and great exhaustion, which leaves the system exposed to disease of various kinds.

Foundation Laid for Various Diseases Later in Life. If the practice is continued from the ages of fifteen and upward, nature will protest against the abuse she has suffered, and continues to suffer, and will make them pay the penalty for the transgression of her laws, especially from the ages of thirty to forty-five, by numerous pains in the system and various dieases, such as affection of the liver and lungs, neuralgia, rheumatism, affection of the spine, diseased kidneys, and cancerous humors. Some of nature's fine machinery gives way, leaving a heavier task for the remaining to perform, which disorders nature's fine arrangement; and there is often a sudden breaking down of the constitution, and death is the result.—CG 444.

The Results of Self-Abuse. Females possess less vital force than the other sex, and are deprived very much of the bracing, invigorating air by their indoor life. The results of self-abuse in them is seen in various diseases such as catarrh, dropsy, headache, loss of memory and sight, great weakness in the back and loins, affections of the spine, the head often decays inwardly. Cancerous humor, which would lie dormant in the system their lifetime, is inflamed and commences its eating, destructive work. The mind is often utterly ruined, and insanity takes place."*—AM 27.

------

*See Appendix A.

One Who Requested Prayer for Healing. My husband and I once attended a meeting where our sympathies were enlisted for a brother who was a great sufferer with the phthisic. He was pale and emaciated. He requested the prayers of the people of God. He said that his family were sick, and that he had lost a child. He spoke with feeling of his bereavement. He said that he had been waiting for some time to see Brother and Sister White. He had believed that if they would pray for him, he would be healed. After the meeting closed, the brethren called our attention to the case. They said that the church was assisting them, that his wife was sick, and his child had died. The brethren had met at his house and united in praying for the afflicted family. We were much worn and had the burden of labor upon us during the meeting and wished to be excused. I had resolved not to engage in prayer for anyone, unless the Spirit of the Lord should dictate in the matter. . . .

That night we bowed in prayer and presented his case before the Lord. We entreated that we might know the will of God concerning him. All we desired was that God might be glorified. Would the Lord have us pray for this afflicted man? We left the burden with the Lord and retired to rest. In a dream the case of that man was clearly presented. His course from his childhood up was shown, and that if we should pray, the Lord would not hear us, for he regarded iniquity in his heart. The next morning the man came for us to pray for him. We took him aside and told him we were sorry to be compelled to refuse his request. I related my dream, which he acknowledged was true. He had practiced self-abuse from his boyhood up, and he had continued the practice during his married life, but said he would try to break himself of it. This man had a long-established habit to overcome. He was in the middle age of life. His moral principles were so weak that when brought in conflict with long-established indulgence, they were overcome. . . .

Here was a man debasing himself daily and yet daring to venture into the presence of God and ask an increase of strength which he had vilely squandered, and which, if granted, he would consume upon his lust. What forbearance has God! If He should deal with man according to his corrupt ways, who could live in His sight? What if we had been less cautious and carried the case of this man before God while he was practicing iniquity, would the Lord have heard? Would He have answered? "For thou art not a God that hath pleasure in wickedness: neither shall evil dwell with Thee. The foolish shall not stand in Thy sight; Thou hatest all workers of iniquity.". . .

This is not a solitary case. Even the marriage relation was not sufficient to preserve this man from the corrupt habits of his youth. I wish I could be convinced that such cases as the one I have presented are rare, but I know they are frequent.—CG 450, 451.

18. Child Abuse

Dear Brother: I have just read your letter dated April 26. May the Lord help me to write you the very words that will be for your restoration and not for your destruction.

I feel sorry, very sorry, for you. Sin, my brother, is sin; it is the transgression of the law, and should I try to lessen that sin before you I would not be doing you any good. You as a Christian receive harm to your own soul. Your whole religious experience is cheapened, and you cannot have faith and trust in God while you have unclean thoughts and defiled hands. The work needs to begin at the soul, and then it will work out in the character. Your mind and heart are polluted, else all such actions would be loathsome. It is a great sin, especially for one who professes to be preaching the gospel of Christ.

I have had this class of sins presented to me as producing moral defilement. What can the impression be upon those youth whose bodies you degrade by your actions? How can you be a shepherd of the sheep and lambs while corrupting their minds, and tainting and polluting their moral sense? Would you consider this matter as lightly as you have done should a minister of the gospel, as Elder W, do such things to your sisters or to your children? This is a crime in the sight of God and I cannot cover it over as a light matter. It is a Sodomitish sin. It is tainting and polluting in all its tendencies, and an abomination in the sight of a holy God. It is practicing iniquity.

Any youth who would submit her body to be handled by a man is in no way fit for the kingdom of heaven. All this vile practice and commonness is what is ruining our youth. Would you practice this upon the body of your own child? Would you not consider it incest, discovering her nakedness? All who do such things are leading young women into abominable practices. I know what these things lead to. To lewdness, lustful practices. Consider how you must dishonor and degrade the truth. Oh, God hates all such sins. How could you do this and at the same time be preaching the Word to sinners—yourself a sinner?

I know how God regards these sins. A married man, a minister of the gospel, leading the lambs of the flock into Sodomitish practices. Now for Christ's sake do not again practice this wicked work and destroy your own soul and the souls of others. It is well that you have not been permitted to continue this awful polluting practice. It is no light sin. The effect upon the mind of the one who submits herself to your touch cannot be measured. Human beings are the Lord's property, and to do any action to corrupt them is a terrible insult to Jesus Christ, who gave His life for these precious souls, that they should not perish in their sins, but have everlasting life, and such actions may ruin the souls for whom Christ has died. Will you continue this work to ruin souls?

Looking unto Jesus who is the Author and Finisher of your faith, you will be of good courage in the Lord. We cannot but know that the end of all things is at hand. I come to you as a physician of souls; I tell you that it is not possible for you to act as a minister. What are you doing? Leading young women to the tree of knowledge of evil practices and teaching them to pluck the fruit which is only evil. This is doing Satan's work most effectually. It is poisoning minds and filling them with unholy imaginings.

These are the very sins which corrupted Sodom. Their evil practices did not come all at once. First one man and woman stupefied themselves by unholy, polluted habits. Then as inhabitants settled in Sodom, they did as you are doing, educating others in a line that is forbidden of God. And so as the inhabitants continued to multiply, these ministers of sin continued in educating them in their own defiling practices until if any person came into their midst their first thoughts were to educate them in their evil work, until Sodom became renowned for its pollutions. Their sins reached unto heaven, and the Lord would bear with them no longer. He destroyed them and all that was beautiful, that made it as a second Eden, for the earth was defiled under the inhabitants thereof.

These bodies that you tamper with are the purchased property of Jesus Christ. I knew this was your sin, but I knew also that if the truth was enthroned in your heart it would make this sin appear to you in its true enormity, for truth brought into the soul temple will expel lust and defilement from the heart. . . .

You say you did not commit adultery. God charges adultery against everyone who doeth these things, and all who will communicate these vile practices to another are polluting that soul with vile imaginations. Can you not see, can you not understand by your own experience, that you are leading youth into this habit of self abuse? You have given them the fruit of the tree of knowledge [of good and evil], and every evil communicated is causing them to partake of the fruit of the tree of knowledge [of good and evil], which God has forbidden to be eaten. . . .

How can I frame words to express the enormity of this awful sin? How can I present it in such a manner that you will no longer look upon it, as you have done, as no great wrong? I have granddaughters, the children of my son, W. C. White. If I were forced to choose whether these children should be exposed to these temptations, educated in these evil practices, or be cut down by death, I would say, Let them die in their innocency. Let them not be corrupted by eating the apples of Sodom. . . .

If you will take hold of Christ by living faith, and humble your soul before Him, He will undertake your case and angels will guard you. But you must resist the devil. You must educate yourself to a different train of thought. Put no confidence in yourself. Never seek the companionship of women or girls. Keep away from them. Your moral taste is so perverted that you will ruin yourself and ruin many souls if you do not turn square about. Educate your mind to study the Word of God. Study it with your whole heart and pray much. Everlasting life is worth a lifelong, persevering, untiring effort. Educate that mind which you have misused and directed in wrong channels of thought.

Educate it to dwell on the life, the character, and the lessons of Christ. . . .

Do not feel that the worst thing for you is to lose your credentials. You are not worthy to be entrusted with the care of the flock. You must know this without my telling you. A little time of probation is still granted you; make the most of it in searching the Word. Every lost blessing is a great loss to you, but if you come into a right position before God you may now receive forgiveness for the past, but do not let your future life have the dark blot of the past. . . .

You ask me if you shall make a public confession. I say, No. Do not dishonor the Master by making public the fact that one ministering in the Word could be guilty of such sin as you have committed. It would be a disgrace to the ministry. Do not give publicity to this matter by any means. It would do injustice to the whole cause of God. It would create impure thoughts in the minds of many even to hear these things repeated. Defile not the lips even by communicating this to your wife, to make her ashamed and bow her head in sorrow. Go to God and to the brethren who know this terrible chapter in your experience and say what you have to say, then let prayer be offered to God in your behalf. Cultivate sobriety. Walk carefully and prayerfully before God. Acquire moral stamina by saying, "I will not dishonor my Redeemer."—Letter 106a, 1896.

Transmitting Messages of Reproof. I am sorry that you feel injured because I let Brother A have a copy of the letter I sent to you. I did not do this to injure you in any way. You had yourself written me that you had made matters known to him concerning yourself and he thought you should confess the whole matter to the church. I thought that letter would prevent any such movement and keep the matter as private as possible.

I do not in any way favor his reading the matter to your mother. She has an abundance of sorrows to carry. I did not sanction any public exposure. I thought that the letter, which condemned the sin, also encouraged you to hope and trust in God. I supposed that it would help Brother A to help you. If it has added to your affliction, making matters any worse for you, I am sincerely sorry.

Whenever I have written a message of reproof, I have always sent one copy to the minister who is officiating in the church, that he may have wisdom to recover such ones as are in danger through temptation, giving them such advice as they need. I also knew, under existing circumstances, that it would not be possible to give you credentials as a shepherd, recommending you to the confidence of the people, because knowing your course of action, if you should in any way be overcome, the Lord would make the conference guilty of the sin of which you are guilty.—Letter 120, 1897.

COUNSELS TO PEOPLE WITH MORAL PROBLEMS

19. A Housewife[2]

Ruin of a Wife's Happiness. My spirit is stirred within me. I cannot hold my peace. Recent developments have caused me anguish of spirit and agony of soul; and then when I think of the misery of poor Sister J, whose happiness you have ruined forever, then I inquire, What will be your reward for these things? We are to be judged according to the deeds done in the body. We feel that it would be just and right for you to be brought to receive the punish-

---

1. This section contains personal testimonies directed mostly to ministerial and institutional workers in the nineteenth-century Seventh-day Adventist Church. Ellen White designed that her counsel to specific individuals should benefit others as well, where similar conditions existed. She wrote:

"When the Lord singles out individual cases and specifies their wrongs, others, who have not been shown in vision, frequently take it for granted that they are right, or nearly so. If one is reproved for a special wrong, brethren and sisters should carefully examine themselves to see wherein they have failed and wherein they have been guilty of the same sin. . . . In rebuking the wrong one, He designs to correct many. . . . He makes plain the wrongs of some that others may thus be warned, and fear, and shun those errors."—2T 112, 113. Concerning the large number of letters in this section that are addressed to ministers of the gospel, the reader is referred to the Preface.

2. A married woman who had become infatuated with another woman's husband to the point of committing adultery.

ment you so justly merit, but we remember the words of Scripture, "Vengeance is Mine; I will repay, saith the Lord." That which you have sown you shall reap. Yes, you will reap a bountiful crop. No frost shall blight it; no mildew blast it; no cankerworm devour it. You have sown to the flesh; you shall reap corruption. A heavy retribution awaits you.

Not only have you sinned against your family and cast a stain upon your children, the fruit of your body, which shall cleave to them like the leprosy, but you have plucked the joy, the happiness, from Sister J's fireside forever.

Have you become so hardened that you have no fear of God, of the judgment, of eternity, when your acts, however secret, are to pass in review before God? Do you realize that your evil doings are faithfully chronicled in heaven, written in the book, and that the Word of God, the statute book, is to judge you in that day?

Eternal Results of Unrepented Adultery. What did God command Moses to do with those who were guilty of adultery? They should be stoned to death. Does the punishment end there? No, they are to die the second death. The stoning system has been done away, but the penalty for transgressing God's law is not done away. If the transgressor does not heartily repent, he will be punished with everlasting destruction from the presence of the Lord.

I hear you have said, "I love Walter J." What business have you to love Walter J, when he belongs to another? Will you ruin and break an innocent wife's heart for the sake of gratifying your guilty love?

Unlawful Relationships in Families. What family is safe if others pursue the heaven-daring course you have? They might just as properly enter into my family, insinuate themselves into my husband's affections, and then tear him from me to satisfy their guilty love. Again I ask you, Are you so hardened that you have no fear of God, of His fierce anger, which will soon come upon the sinner, unmixed with mercy? You are willing to sell your soul cheap, disgrace your brother, disgrace your children, to satisfy your lustful heart.

After you have gotten Walter J, what then? You have a man who fears not to break God's law, who fears not to break the heart of a kind wife who has borne him many children and laid them in the grave—a wife who has given him the warmth of her affections in youth—a wife he has lived with until they are on the decline of life! Think you after you get this Walter J for yourself entirely, after you steal him from the wife of his youth, he will ever remain constant and true to you who have accomplished so much evil to satisfy your guilty love?

The truth found Walter J a hard case. It has done everything for him. Now he has no fear of God, no fear of transgressing His law. Evil angels take charge of his mind and yours, and then how constant and true and even will your love run? You have sowed to yourself misery, misery. Evermore will a guilty conscience haunt you. Is it possible now for you to retrace your steps? Is it possible that a merciful God would pity you yet?

How dare you love Walter J, and add to your sin that of breaking his wife's heart? Oh, you have sold heaven very cheap. You have shown what is your choice. Your life has marked your choice, that of being outside the city, with dogs, sorcerers, adulterers, whoremongers, and those who love and make a lie.

Please read Proverbs 6, twentieth verse and onward. Read Revelation, chapter 7.—Letter 12, 1864.

20. A Long-standing Adventist and His Mistress

To One Far Gone in Disobedience. My poor, deceived, sinful brother, I will now address a few words to you for whom I have had so great a burden and interest for many years. Ira K, for years your course has been a sinful course. I have written to you but have received no response, and the reproof given has had no effect upon your course of action. . . .

You have a work to do for your own soul. Make haste, or it will be forever too late. God will now forgive the scarlet sin if you will do those things you ought to do to make your wrongs right. I do not say your case is hopeless, but you have certainly almost sinned away your day of grace; and yet Jesus is in the sanctuary. Jesus pleads in your behalf. Your brethren and your sisters have labored much for you; so much interest have they manifested for you that you have regarded crime and sins as a light matter. But Jesus loves you, and I present or lift up Jesus before you.

Satan tells you that it is not best for you to cease sinning; you have gone so far in disobedience and transgression that it is no use for you to try to come back to God. While I feel that full disgrace of your sins is upon you, while I would have you see sin as it is, I would all the time present Jesus as a sin-pardoning Saviour.

Eleventh-hour Pardon. The sands of your life are nearly run out, and now if you will come to God just as you are, without one plea but that He has died to save the chiefest of sinners, you will find pardon even in this the eleventh hour. Man must cooperate with God. Christ did not die to have the power to cover transgression unrepented of and unconfessed. Not all sins are to be confessed publicly, but some are to be confessed alone to God and the parties that have been injured.

Christ's Imputed Righteousness. The righteousness of Christ imputed to men means holiness, uprightness, purity. Unless Christ's righteousness was imputed to us we could not have acceptable repentance. The righteousness dwelling in us by faith consists of love, forbearance, meekness, and all the Christian virtues. Here the righteousness of Christ is laid hold of and becomes a part of our being. All who have this righteousness will work the works of God. . . .

But the robes of Christ's righteousness never cover cherished sins. No one can enter into the marriage supper of the Lamb without the wedding garment on, which is the righteousness of Christ. Without holiness no man shall see God. God is waiting to give divine power to every soul to combine with human effort. "Work out your own salvation with fear and trembling, for it is God that worketh in you, both to will and to do of His good pleasure."

Christ is the perfection of divine character. He is the model we are to follow. Peter's words are full of meaning: "As obedient children, not fashioning yourselves according to the former lusts in your ignorance; but as He which hath called you is holy, so be ye holy in all manner of conversation; because it is written, Be ye holy; for I am holy" [1 Peter 1:14-16]. . . .

Names in the Book of Life. John in Revelation, in his description of the New Jerusalem, says, "And there shall in no wise enter into it any thing that defileth, neither whatsoever worketh abomination, or maketh a lie: but they which are written in the Lamb's book of life" [Rev. 21:27]. Well may you ask, "Is my name written there?" It is registered in that book of life if you have a character that is pure and holy like the character of Christ. Faith in the truth alone will not save us. We must be like Christ if we shall one day see Him as He is.

"Every man that hath this hope in him purifieth himself even as He is pure." Any hope aside and separate from purity and righteousness is a snare of Satan, sophistry, and fatal delusion. Jesus came to our world, and graciously stands inviting us to come unto Him and learn of Him, believe in Him; and as we come, He grafts us into His life and into His character. Our drawing nigh to Christ is faith, and the grafting process is adoption; and by this mutual act we become sons of God and joint heirs with Christ, partakers of the divine nature, having escaped the corruption that is in the world through lust.

Grafts Into Christ. This ingrafting in Christ separates us from the world. No longer will we love the society of the vile and contaminated and contaminating. We will be dead indeed unto sin, but alive unto God through Jesus Christ our Lord. Then rich clusters of fruit are borne. The graces of the Spirit are borne in love, joy, peace, longsuffering, gentleness, goodness. We have new affections, new appetites, new tastes. Old things have passed away, and lo, all things have become new.

A Life or Death Choice. Now I ask you, Brother K, will you serve God with your whole heart, keeping all His commandments, or will you serve the devil? Will you, irrespective of consequences, put yourself on Christ's side? God will not force your service. It is life or death with you. If you come to Jesus, confessing your sins as a humble penitent, He will forgive you your sins and cleanse you from all unrighteousness. You cannot turn from sin until you hate sin and love purity and truth and righteousness. I entreat you now to come just as a little child, humbling your heart before God, and Jesus will pardon your transgression.

Society of the Ungodly. I hope Annie will no longer hold the influence over you that she has. If she does, it is ruin, eternal ruin, to you both. You have much, altogether too much, sympathy while your wife is wronged, deceived, robbed of the respect due her, your children robbed of that confidence which you should give them, to give to aliens. You have a work to do, and that without delay, or the wages of sin will be your portion.

Turn away from the society of the ungodly; devote every moment of your time in seeking the Lord while He may be found. You cannot live two lives, one for Christ and one for the devil. How long will you delight in sin itself, which is so abhorrent to God? All the sweet influences of the Spirit of God have become extinguished in your soul. Now change. I tell you not to be despairing, but to come to a merciful, sin-pardoning Saviour. Sever the links; disconnect from them.

You tremble to do this because you fear exposure. You cannot but be exposed ere long, however much you may conceal your true condition. God has opened matters to me that I might encourage you to make another trial for your soul. You must choose between selfishness and sin on the one hand, and Christ, His purity and righteousness, on the other. If you surrender to God heart, soul, and body you will no longer be the servant of sin. Oh, I cannot endure the thought that one who has had so great light shall remain the servant of sin and of Satan.

Entire Transformation. There is no hope for you except in an entire transformation of character. Then you will try to honor Christ and to be like Christ. His law will be the rule of your life. Make haste to turn your feet in the path of holiness. Save your soul by casting yourself at the foot of the cross. Then come to Jesus and be happy, and go to heaven. Preaching is not all you need, but you need sins rebuked as Nathan rebuked David. "Thou art the man." You must have godliness, a pure heart, a perfect life, or die in your sins and perish with the ungodly.

May the Lord convince your soul, is my prayer.—Letter 1e, 1890.

Message to a Mistress. I have a few words to write to you. For some years your course has been open before me in connection with the family of Ira K, but these are hidden chapters in the experience of you both, which may have been surmised by some, that have been binding you together in unholy companionship. I hear that you and your brother have been converted; and if this report is true, you will bring forth fruit meet for repentance. "He that covereth his sins shall not prosper."

You have held a strong influence over Ira K. Your connection with him has been of that character that you well know, unless repented of and confessed, you will never see the kingdom of heaven. Can you sell your soul so cheaply? Is it possible that sin has lost it's hideousness to you? I have not the slightest confidence in him whom I have long called Brother K.

His course has been opened before me in plain, distinct lines. No one knows that which I know of the wretched past. I never meant anyone should know of it, but the end of Ira K's life is not far off, and shall he go into eternity with his sins unconfessed, unrepented of? What will you say when you shall stand before the judgment bar of God?

Does Sin Appear Sinful? He has so long been following the impulses of his own corrupt heart that sin does not appear to him exceedingly sinful. Now, as your thoughts have been awakened to the serious thoughts of the salvation of your soul, I hope you see the hatefulness of sin; I hope you will now confess your sins before it shall be forever too late. If Ira K dies as he is now, fastened in iniquity, what will you both have to meet in the judgment? Your course has been a sad and distressing course in this matter. Did you think that God did not see these things? . . .

God's eye has been upon you. He has marked your deceptive course. You have alienated the affections of Ira K from his long-suffering wife. You have held your influence over Ira K, and he dare not break it; he dare not displease you. . . . You have, like the archdeceiver, framed lies, and have worked upon a mind that was degraded and cheapened and perverted by his own sin to make him view things in altogether a distorted light.

Now, if God has touched your heart, as I sincerely hope He has, you will humble your heart, you will fall upon the Rock and be broken. You will confess your sins, and forever forsake them, and begin a new life. You will now have things brought to your remembrance in regard to your course of action toward a worn, burdened child of God— Sister K. She has had her faults, but she has not despised reproof. She has ever been ready to bow to the light and will of God.

But as your case has been opened before me, and as your sins have been pointed out to me, I have kept them to myself, hoping that a time would come when your hard spirit might be softened. I now implore you to seek the salvation of your soul before it shall be forever too late. The sins of fault-finding with Sister K are light in comparison with your sin and that of her husband. You have both been weaving a net about yourselves that has been growing firm as bands of steel, but the judgments of God will not be long deferred if you continue on in the way you have been.

God's Forbearance, Then God's Wrath. God keeps a

record of the sins of nations and of individuals, and when they have reached a certain measure they are full; then when the long forbearance of God is exhausted, His wrath slumbereth not. If necessary, I can show you the reproofs given Ira K. I can no longer call him Brother, for he is not a Christian. I have labored to keep him from the depths of despair, all the time hoping that he would see the evil of his course, that he would repent before he had grieved away the last ray of the mercy of God forever.

But I have been shown that he sets his mind and heart against right doing and receives your cruel influence as truth. You have helped him to turn from those who are his true friends, who would exert an influence to save his soul. It is time for me to speak. Ira K does not want me to come to his home. He does not want me near him, for he fears God will rebuke his wicked course, and yours.

I dare not keep these things from you. I hope you will now seek the Lord with your whole heart, that you may find Him. Better go in humility all the rest of your life than to lose your own soul and be the means of other souls being lost through your course of action. Sin does not appear exceeding sinful to you, but God says, "I know thy works." So every deception you have practiced, every false word you have uttered, and to every unholy action there has been a watcher from whom you could not exclude yourself.

At Belshazzar's Feast. Little did Belshazzar think on that night of that sacrilegious feast that there was a messenger from heaven watching his every movement; and that night the performance in that palace brought the figures of his evil works to their full measure. He was no longer to be protected and shielded by God. The restraining power was no longer to ward off the evil; he was to fall, his kingdom was to pass into other hands, and his body was to be slain.

Appeals From God's Word. My heart is full of sadness. I inquire, Must these souls be left to come up in the second resurrection; left to be outside the city of God among dogs and sorcerers and adulterers and those who "loveth and maketh a lie"? What can I say to you? You have a strong, hard spirit, unless you have fallen upon the Rock and are broken.

The Lord has said, "Come now, and let us reason together: . . . though your sins be as scarlet, they shall be as white as snow; though they be red like crimson, they shall be as wool" [Isa. 1:18]. "Seek ye the Lord while He may be found, call ye upon Him while He is near: Let the wicked forsake his way, and the unrighteous man his thoughts: and let him return unto the Lord, and He will have mercy upon him; and to our God, for He will abundantly pardon" [Isa. 55:6, 7]. "If we confess our sins, He is faithful and just to forgive us our sins, and to cleanse us from all unrighteousness. If we say that we have not sinned, we make Him a liar, and His word is not in us" [1 John 1:9, 10].

I beseech of you, let the work go deep; make thorough work. In the place of carrying your supposed grievances to Ira K, a poor, erring, sinful mortal, to obtain sympathy, take your grievances to Jesus. He has invited you, "Come unto Me, all ye that labor and are heavy laden, and I will give you rest. Take My yoke upon you, and learn of Me; for I am meek and lowly in heart; and ye shall find rest unto your souls. For My yoke is easy, and My burden is light" [Matt. 11:28-30].—Letter 23a, 1890.

Another Message to the Mistress. I again address you not to fail in this time which is the crisis of your life, to take the only right course left for you to take. The stronghold of sin is in the will. Put your will on God's side of the question;

place yourself no longer in the position of a sinner, a harlot. You may not see clearly how you will obtain deliverance from the sins which have been cherished, and strengthened with repetition. The only way is to confess your sins, forsake them, and believe that Jesus will pardon you.

Your deliverance is to be found in Christ, and Him alone. Your temper and your pride must die, and Christ live in you, else you are still in the bondage of sin and iniquity. You must humble your heart before God, and Jesus will pity and save you. . . .

If you desire to be a Christian, now is your time; now is the golden opportunity. You can walk in purity only by looking and beholding, praying and believing in Jesus moment by moment. You have been living in adultery so long that sin does not appear heinous to you. You love sin. If now you want to leave sin, you must forever renounce it. If you confess your sins, He is faithful and just to forgive you your sins, and to cleanse you from all unrighteousness. You must not hide or excuse your sins, but you must arise and make haste to confess your sins, and save your soul by seeking the forgiveness of your sins.

Evil Influence of Family Members. Oh, it is a terrible thing to be lost. Your course has been a sad and distressing one. Time is short. Will you now come? Will you sit at the feet of Jesus, and learn of Him? There is hope for you, but you have had miserable counselors, and if you love Jesus you hate the evil course, and even the conversation and companionship, of your own relatives who have given themselves soul, body, and spirit to work the works of Satan. He has control of their imaginations and evil intentions to do wickedly.

May the Lord send most deep convictions to your soul, for I never want to give publicity to the things which I have been shown; and I hope you will take a course which will make it unnecessary for me to do this.—Letter 24a, 1890.

A Second Letter to Ira K. Today I have just received your response to my letter, and I cannot rest tonight without writing to you again and saying, "Repent of your sins without delay." Your course has been opened before me; your management in business, your reckless expenditure of money, your associations with the vile and corrupt; and yet God is willing to pardon even you. . . .

Had it not been for your unlawful, unholy connection with Miss L, you would not have pursued so unnatural a course toward your own children. You have felt hard and unreconciled with [your daughter] Lucinda, but clung all the time to a harlot, and your commerce with her was of that character that your God-fearing children had none of your love, your sympathy. But my letter is not to condemn you, but to awaken you to repentance. I hear Anna has professed to be converted. This is the only time I dared to write to you or to her, knowing it would not do a bit of good, for the hardness of both your hearts and your stubbornness to pursue an evil course have been marvelous.

Jesus, Only Hope of Sinners. The bewitching power of Satan has been upon you. But make no delay; Jesus is at the right hand of God and mercy still lingers. "Come now," says the Lord, "and let us reason together; . . . though your sins be as scarlet, they shall be as white as snow; though they be red like crimson, they shall be as wool" [Isa. 1:18]. Yes, Jesus is the sinner's only hope. "Ho, every one that thirsteth, come ye to the waters, and he that hath no money (no goodness, no righteousness, nothing to recommend him to God); come ye, buy, and eat; yea, come, buy wine and milk without money and without price" [Isa. 55:1].

Cannot you come just now, just as you are, saying, "In my hand no price I bring, simply to Thy cross I cling"? "Wherefore do ye spend money for that which is not bread? and your labor for that which satisfieth not? hearken diligently unto Me, and eat ye that which is good, and let your soul delight itself in fatness. Incline your ear, and come unto Me: hear, and your soul shall live; and I will make an everlasting covenant with you, even the sure mercies of David" [verses 2, 3]. . . .

A Change of Heart Versus Suicide. Consider these words: "And I saw the dead, small and great, stand before God; and the books were opened; and another book was opened: . . . and the dead were judged out of those things which were written in the books, according to their works." "And whosoever was not found written in the book of life was cast into the lake of fire." [Rev. 20:12, 15.]

Do not, I entreat of you, sit down in hopeless despair and do nothing. Do not heed any further the great tempter, that it is no use for you to try. You could but perish if you came to Jesus just as you are, sinful and polluted, vile and depraved; but Jesus is amply able to save the very hardest and the most wicked and defiled sinner.

You say you are tempted to cut the brittle thread of life; but if you do, then your case is hopeless, for you add the sin of murder to all your other sins. But if you come just as you are, helpless and sin-polluted, and cast yourself at the foot of the cross, poor, miserable, blind, and naked, there is a Saviour to lift you up. I know that you have not for many, many years been in harmony with God. You have for a long stretch of years been following another leader, which is the prince of darkness; but if you will cast off the works of darkness, if you will now look unto Jesus, you will live.

Prayers in Behalf of Sinners. But you must look in faith. The true Christian life you have known nothing of for years; but while your powers have been so wasted and you have served Satan with a high hand, the Lord has heard prayer in your behalf, and has not cut you off in your sins, which He might easily have done if mercy were gone forever. Yes, God has heard the prayers of those whom you have refused to connect with, those who love God and keep the commandments. You have been utterly blind, deplorably deceived, deluded, and ensnared by the devil. . . .

Another Chance. Now year after year is gone, and God gives you through His delegated servant another chance. Will you repent? Will you confess your sins and forsake them? If you arouse your will power, relying wholly on the strength of Jesus, you will yet be an overcomer; but, let the consequences be what they will, you must separate entirely from the class you have associated with. . . .

I cannot give you up to be lost. You have been blind to all the higher interests of the soul, to all the blessed, glorious attractions of a heavenly life in the city of God. You have labored for that which is not bread; you have sacrificed peace and honor, and sacrificed the companionship of the children of God, even your own children, that you might walk without obstructions in your own way. You have striven to content yourself in the secrets of sinful pleasure and base gratifications, irrespective of God and heaven, and yet Jesus offers you that which you most need, that which is of infinite gain, even if it cost the toil and suffering of a whole lifetime.

Hope for One With a Hardened Conscience. Now you have no hope; you are without God; and yet Jesus of Nazareth passeth by. Will you now cry to God with a broken, repentant heart, "Jesus of Nazareth, have mercy on me"? I press this matter upon your conscience. May God urge it upon your soul with arguments of mighty power. Oh, that the blind might see the solemnity of eternal judgment, and deepen the appeal I make to you at this time. I am writing in the early morning hours, while all in the house are locked in slumber. Be not determined to be lost. You cannot comprehend what a terrible thing it is to be lost. Your conscience has become hardened in sin and transgression and unbelief; but you may, if you will, fall on the Rock Christ Jesus and be broken before it is utterly too late, crying, "Jesus of Nazareth, have mercy on me." If you do this, God will not leave you to perish. . . .

Whatever suggestions Satan may make to keep your soul bound in sin and despair, I still say, Go to Jesus, the sin-pardoning Saviour, without delay. And may the Lord who is mighty to save rescue you out of the snare of the devil, is my prayer.—Letter 1d, 1890.

21. A Hospital Worker

Frivolous, Unwise Attention to Women. Angels of God are watching the development of character. Angels of God are weighing moral worth. If you bestow your attentions upon those who have no need, you are doing the recipients harm, and you will receive condemnation rather than reward. Remember that, when by your trifling conversation you descend to the level of frivolous characters, you are encouraging them in the path that leads to perdition. Your unwise attentions may prove the ruin of their souls. You degrade their conceptions of what constitutes Christian life and character. You confuse their ideas, and make impressions that can never be effaced.

The harm thus done to souls that need to be strengthened, refined, ennobled, is often a sin unto death.

They cannot associate these men with the sacred positions they occupy. The ministers, the officers of the church, are all regarded as no better than themselves. Then where is their example?

God's Pure Standard. God calls upon all who claim to be Christians to elevate the standard of righteousness, and to purify themselves even as Christ is pure. . . .

The question is, Shall we be Bible Christians? Will we disregard the plainest instruction given us in the Word of Life, and erect a false standard whereby to measure our character? Is this a safe thing for us to do? When you yield to the temptations of the enemy, and do the very opposite of that which God has instructed you to do, and then excuse yourselves, saying that you meant no harm, that you have done no moral wrong, what can be your standard of piety and holiness? Christ has given us the signs whereby we may distinguish the genuine Christian; no one need be deceived by the pretentious claims of the hypocrite.

No Excuse for Flirting. There is no excuse for indulging a love-sick sentimentalism; no excuse for this trifling, flirting of married men with young girls, or married men with widows. Let men professing godliness heed the apostle's admonition, "Dearly beloved, I beseech you as strangers and pilgrims, abstain from fleshly lusts, which war against the soul; having your conversation honest among the Gentiles: that, whereas they speak evil against you as evildoers, they may by your good works, which they shall behold, glorify God in the day of visitation" [1 Peter 2:11, 12].

Will you, then, disregard the plainest directions given in the Word of God in regard to your words, your deportment, and your character? Will you excuse levity, and even licentious acts, as though you had done no moral wrong? Will you pass all this off by saying it was thoughtlessness on your part? Is it not the duty of Christians to think soberly? If Jesus is enthroned in the heart, will the thoughts be running riot? . . .

Example of the Antediluvians. We have the history of the antediluvians and of the [inhabitants of the] cities of the plains, whose course of conduct degenerated from lightness and frivolity to debasing sins which called forth the wrath of God in a most dreadful destruction, in order to rid the earth of the curse of their contaminating influence. Inclination and passion bore sway over reason. Self was their god, and the knowledge of the Most High was nearly obliterated through a selfish indulgence of corrupt passions.—Letter 84, 1888.

22. A Sanitarium Superintendent*

Equal Guilt of Two Persons. In the night season I saw you in the company of the matron of the institution. As far as your attentions to each other were concerned, you might have been man and wife. Your conduct toward each other was wrong in the sight of God, and my heart was grieved by the condition of things. I asked, "Who hath bewitched you, that ye should not obey the truth?" God is displeased. You have grieved His Holy Spirit. Sister N will never again be what she once was. Both of you are guilty before God.— Letter 30, 1887 (written June 11, 1887).

Ministers Not Above Suspicion and Temptation. Elder M has been very imprudent with Mrs. or Sister N, and I have

---

*This man, an ordained minister, had been a widower for about five years when these letters were written. The occasionl blanks are reproduced as they appear in the file copies of the letters in the White Estate vault.

handled this familiarity with decision in the fear of God, under a great burden. He stated that it was his privilege for the superintendent to ride with the matron; and he told me, quite aggrieved, that the church members had much talk of his always taking Sister N to the meeting; and when the matter came up in the camp meeting at Oakland in the presence of about twenty, he justified himself that he had, he said, been spoken to in regard to Sister N riding with him and her husband not being with them, but he knew that this was no moral wrong, and therefore he went on just the same.

I just arose and told him plainly he was not a Bible Christian; that the Word of the Lord was positive, abstaining from the very appearance of evil and to give no action [or] reproach to fall upon the cause of God. But, knowing that much talk was being made over his close association with another man's wife, he had not sought in his own course of action to cut off the reproach, but justified his course. Had he seen another man taking the same liberties with his wife when she was living, he would have felt indignant. Had he seen any of the men connected with the institution, young or old, thus intimate with a married woman or young girls, he would have seen the evil and with no soothing words would have made short work of this matter.

He stated he should have done so, but that he considered he was a minister, above suspicion and above temptation, he had thought, and therefore it was safe for him to do that which would be sin in another. He acknowledged that this was wrong reasoning, but every time the matter was talked upon he brought forward excuses.—Letter 53, 1888 (written Feb. 10, 1888).

No Confession, No Conversion. Dear Brother Church: You may say, Has the Lord shown you this peculiar case of Elder M and Mrs. N?

If I had my diary here, written during my last trip to Denmark, Norway, and Sweden, I could read to you some things therein. In a vision of the night I was passing through the rooms of the institution, and saw the very scenes which did take place there in this familiarity, men with women and women with men. My soul was deeply troubled, and I arose and wrote out these things at one o'clock in the morning. . . .

I was shown at a certain time when the Spirit of the Lord was working upon those connected with the institution, some confessions were made. They seemed to be assembled in a meeting of worship. Elder M was standing upon his feet, and the Spirit of God was deeply moving upon his heart to confess his way out of darkness into the light. But he spoke only in general terms. He in no wise cleared his soul from the stains of wrong on his part in connection with Sister N. He trembled for a while under the prompting of the Spirit of God, but refused to humiliate his soul before God in lifting the cross.

A Diverging Path With Satan as Leader. From that time he began to walk in darkness, contrary to light and truth. He had a molding influence upon Sister N. She felt at one time that she could never be free, unless she made a humble confession. But Elder M molded matters to please himself. He might have made straightforward work; he might have come out of darkness into the light; he might have drawn near to God; and the Lord would have forgiven his sins, and lifted up a standard for him against the enemy. But he has verily turned away from the light and the convictions of the Spirit of God, as did the assembly of the Jews at Nazareth, when Christ announced Himself as the Anointed One. . . . It is a dangerous thing under circumstances like these to open the heart to unbelief, which causes the Spirit of God to depart. . . .

It is Satan's constant work to lead minds to deny the light. It takes but a step to leave the straightforward path, and enter a diverging path where Satan leads the way.—Letter 33, 1888 (written March 21, 1888).

Healing From Sin's Wound. Dear Brother M: I have had much burden of soul in your behalf, but at the same time strong confidence in God that He would on this occasion lead you to see your mistakes and errors. I so much desire that you, for your sake and for Christ's sake, should so humble your heart by confessing your sins, that the burden shall be lifted from your soul, and the prayers of your brethren be united with your prayers, and you be healed from the wound sin has made. . . .

My brother, you have walked away from the light into dark places. When I was laboring with you so earnestly, when in an agony of distress in your behalf in _____, oh, why did you not there pity me as well as yourself? Why did you not lift this soul-crushing burden from my heart by acknowledging your sins? Why did you not consider Jesus who was being by you pierced afresh and put to open shame? Why did you deny Christ? Oh, my brother, my soul feels deeply for you! I urged home upon you the light in which your case was presented to me, and I am not exaggerating when I tell you that my soul was wrung with anguish. Why did you stand back, as if unimpressed?

Need of True Repentance. Why did you justify yourself at every point, and let this weight press heavier and heavier upon your own soul, and bring so heavy labor upon me? Why manifest this cold, icy hesitancy to acknowledge your wrongs? Is the high standard of God's holy law too severe? Is the self-denial, the lofty purity of thought that is demanded, too much of a constraint, too irksome to be endured? No requirement is given you which it will not increase your happiness to obey. I know you are suffering. I know you are not happy, and I suffer with you, because you are a member of the body of Christ.

You have enjoyed the love of Jesus, the peace of Christ, in large measure. Most terrible doubts and waverings are torturing your soul. Why not submit to God? Why encase your soul in barriers that will not let the light in? Will my brother see and appreciate the value of his own soul and Christ's work that the gift of eternal life might be placed within his reach? There is great power in the atonement. Your mind is troubled, and the whole soul is in desperate need of a physician.

I cannot give you up. I must see you what God would have you to be, filled with repentance and remorse, which will be followed by a sweet sense of pardon and pure, holy joy. Jesus is sorry for you; He pities you; He wants to save you. He is not willing that you should perish but that you should have eternal life.

God's Law the Only Standard of Righteousness. God has not separated from you, but your sins and your iniquities have separated your soul from God. You are sin-sick, and you need a physician. Look into the mirror, God's holy law, which is the only standard of righteousness. It is the sin detector. Will you see your sins in the light of the law? Will you have faith in Jesus as the sin-pardoning Saviour? The royal law is before you, and you must meet its requirements. It is the only standard of righteousness; it measures your life and your character. I am sad to be compelled to tell you that you are a transgressor of the law. Practical faith in Jesus Christ is the only thing that will save you; the precious blood of Jesus alone will cleanse from every spot and stain of sin.

A Vivid Vision of Adultery. While in Europe the things that transpired in _____ were opened before me. A voice said, "Follow me, and I will show you the sins that are practiced by those who stand in responsible positions." I went through the rooms, and I saw you, a watchman upon the walls of Zion, were very intimate with another man's wife, betraying sacred trusts, crucifying your Lord afresh. Did you consider that there was a Watcher, the Holy One, who was witnessing your evil work, seeing your actions and hearing your words, and these are also registered in the books of heaven?

She was sitting on your lap; you were kissing her, and she was kissing you. Other scenes of fondness, sensual looks and deportment, were presented before me, which sent a thrill of horror through my soul. Your arm encircled her waist, and the fondness expressed was having a bewitching influence. Then a curtain was lifted, and I was shown you in bed with Sister N. My guide said, "Iniquity, adultery.". . .

Unimpressible as a Stone. When I tried to show you the aggravated character of sin in the sight of God of a watchman upon the walls of Zion, you did not seem to feel or to sense the sin, but you seemed as unimpressible as a stone. I know you are seeking to cover your ways from the Lord. I did not then open them to you, as I have done now, with my pen. And I do not wish to have this opened to others, for I do hope that you will see and sense the evil and confess your sin to God and to your brethren and make clean work, that you may have this foul blot removed from you by the cleansing blood of Jesus Christ. You have not confessed your wrongs. You have done great wickedness; you have committed adultery, broken the seventh commandment.

I have carried this heavy load upon my soul all this time. When we had the meetings in _____, you knew just what you ought to confess. You knew the warnings were sent of God; you knew the communications I sent to you from Europe were truth. And when I carried the burdens until my soul seemed crushed, you obtained [the] sympathy of your friends by leaving the impression upon their minds that I was not just, but partial, and very severe; that you were suffering under accusations which were very difficult to bear; that the testimonies I had given were my own judgment, my own words; that I had wronged you; and that false reports had been brought to me. But my brother, nothing could be more deceptive than this. . . .

Doubts Upon Satan's Hooks. I showed you that your position as a minister of the gospel would make any such course as you had pursued a reproach to the cause of God, a matter of scandal, and your actions a savor of death rather than of life. When the standard-bearer falls, who will fight? When the cross is torn down by the ones who should point it out, whom will you believe? What can be more dreadful than a minister of Jesus Christ a commandment breaker? I see only one way for your escape—break with the temptations of Satan at once, and rush for the light! Even ministers who claim to believe the truth are only blind guides if the truth is not enthroned in the heart, and a thorough transition from darkness to light has [not] taken place. They are clouds without water. I urge upon you, if you care for your own eternal welfare, the positive necessity of having the truth enthroned in your heart, for then its principles will sanctify your character. . . .

You have talked over matters as you viewed them, that the communications from Sister White are not all from the Lord, but a portion is her own mind, her own judgment, which is no better than anybody else's judgment and ideas. This is one of Satan's hooks to hang your doubts upon to deceive your soul and the souls of others who will dare to draw the line in this matter and say, This portion which pleases me is from God, but that portion which points out and condemns my course of conduct is from Sister White alone, and bears not the holy signet. You have in this way virtually rejected the whole of the messages, which God in His tender, pitying love has sent to you to save you from moral ruin.

The Truth Which Condemns. God presents to you His will and ways which are in marked contrast in just that which your case requires, and you are hereby tested whether you will accept the reproof, fall on the Rock and be broken, or will you become vexed over plain statements that come close to your soul, because it [the reproof] is the truth and condemns you, and then you feel at enmity with me. Hebrews 4:12. There is One back of me which is the Lord who has prompted the message, which you now reject, and disregard, and dishonor. By tempting God you have unnerved yourself, and confusion and blindness of mind have been the result. A fierce determination has sprung up in your heart in a spirit of defiance to brave it through. . . .

You have a work to do for your soul that no one else can do for you. Your course of error and wrong has been the means of helping others in the same direction. You were never alone. The same hand that traced the characters over against the wall of Belshazzar's palace was registering in the books of heaven the deeds and words that made Christ ashamed of you. You had no respectful courtesy for those whom you should have treated with respect and to whose wants you should have been attentive. These unholy things unfitted you to do the work of the Lord; but in your unholy hands you took your Bible and led the worship, and as mouthpiece for God you were foremost to preach to the people. Where was your conscience? Where was your humility? Where was your fear of God? Where was your faithful work to keep the Health Retreat up to the highest standard?—Letter 16, 1888 (written April 30, 1888).

The Lord Lives. We had a private meeting where humble confessions were made by Elder M and Brother and Sister N. . . .

Well, the Lord lives. I have had a hard battle and some precious victories gained. Elder M is clothed and in his right mind, humble, tender, and broken before God. Humble as a child. I see no way but to keep bearing the plain testimony in love, in patience.—Letter 27, 1888 (written May 29, 1888).

23. A Would-be Sanitarium Superintendent

Separation From Family Not Wise. Brother O: I must say some things to you, for your course is worthy of censure. You know what has been the course of Elder M and others connected with the Health Institute, and how difficult it has been to remove the impression once made. You know the history of the past and the reproach and disgrace that still cling to the institution, and the people at St. Helena are not ignorant of the great curse which fell upon it in consequence of the moral conduct of some who have been connected with it.

I cannot feel that it would be wisdom for you to act in the capacity of superintendent of the Health Institution, for you are not a wise man. You are here away from your wife and family when you should be with them; but if there are reasons to justify this separation, your course should be altogether different than it has been. If you had the sanctifying influence of the grace of Christ in your heart, you would take heed to your own ways and abstain from every appearance of evil.

Your work has been such as to open to many souls the door of temptation, and many will be lost in consequence. You may reform, you may see your mistakes, but you will never be able to remove the impression that has been made.

Reproof for Familiarity With the Opposite Sex. Brother O, you are watched with critical eyes. Your attention to young ladies is not called for. You are out of place in giving so much attention to the P family. Mrs. P has done her work in ruining one good man. That matter was opened before me as an open book. I was told in the night season that you were not qualified to be entrusted with large or even limited responsibilities unless you repent and become a reformed man. God cannot be with you while you pursue this course. My guide told me to follow, and I was shown your boyish familiarity with girls, and your particular sympathy toward Mrs. P and her daughters. The mother keeps [to] the bed much of the time when she should be engaged in some useful employment in the care of her family.

Your familiarities with the mother and daughters were opened before me. Your attentions and your gifts speak louder than even your flattering words. You are displeasing God, and Heaven looks upon you with reproof. . . . Had you a new heart, your motives, actions, and course of conduct would be such that both believers and unbelievers might have an example of a Christlike character. I have seen your case as God sees it, and I now present it to you. Better, far better, would it have been had you disconnected from the Health Retreat some months ago.

This freedom and gallantry toward young ladies is not

the outgrowth of a tender, Christlike sympathy. . . . If you look upon these matters as unworthy of mention, you will repeat them. Investigate your past life, and let moral taste be created by a purification of the soul temple. Put away your excuses, for you have none. Your ideas need a moral renovation, and then you will see things in a different light. God calls for men to do this work who are pure in heart and undefiled in thought, having an eye single to His glory. . . .

Religion Not a Mere Cloak. God sees the heart, the deeds, and the purposes of the mind. It should be written on the conscience as with a pen of iron upon a rock that the man who expects true success in violating the eternal principles of right as written in the books of heaven, is not only foolish but wicked. Can men forget, "Thou God seest me"? Will you, my brother, turn away from idols? Your moral sense is clouded. Pray to God to bring all things to your remembrance that you may see things in their true bearing. Wear not the religion of Christ as a cloak, but put on the Lord Jesus Christ.

Tests of a True Christian. The conversation of the man who claims to believe the truth for this time should be in heaven, not common, earthly, cheap, sensual. Holy maxims must be adopted or that man will walk contrary to Christ, deceiving the world, betraying the truth. Why, oh, why do professed Christians keep so low a level when they have so pure and perfect a gospel?

Watch your religion with a jealous care, and let the word of God dwell in you richly. Let the question be asked, Am I a Christian? Do I love my neighbor as myself? Do I observe the golden rule, to do unto others as I would that they do unto me? Can I be a Christian, and taint and pollute my soul with sinful, corrupting imaginings? It was sin that crucified the Redeemer of the world. Seemingly upright men do strange things, utterly contrary to the oracles of God. Their righteousness is a pretense before Him who looks into the heart. We are not to study and plan for our own interest, but in keeping our souls pure give an example to the youth and to all with whom we associate.—Letter 5, 1890.

24. A Medical Doctor

Wrong Ideas About the Marriage Relation. Dr. Q, your mind has not been healthfully exercised at all times, since you came to the Health Retreat. Your ideas in regard to the marriage relation have been erroneous. Nothing but the violation of the marriage bed can either break or annul the marriage vow. We are living in perilous times, when there is no assurance in anything, save in firm, unwavering faith in Jesus Christ. There is no heart that may not be estranged from God through the devices of Satan, if one does not watch unto prayer.

Your health would have been in a far better condition had your mind been at peace and rest; but it became confused and unbalanced, and you reasoned incorrectly in regard to the matter of divorce. Your views cannot be sustained on the ground from which you reason. Men are not at liberty to make a standard of law for themselves to avoid God's law, and please their own inclination. They must come to God's great moral standard of righteousness.

If the wife is an unbeliever and an opposer, the husband cannot, in view of the law of God, put her away on this ground alone. In order to be in harmony with the law of Jehovah, he must abide with her, unless she chooses of herself to depart. He may suffer opposition and be oppressed and annoyed in many ways; he will find his comfort and his strength and support from God, who is able to give grace for every emergency. He should be a man of pure mind, of truly decided, firm principles, and God will give him wisdom in regard to the course which he should pursue. Impulse will not control his reason, but reason will hold the lines of control in her firm hand, that lust shall be held under bit and bridle.

Marriage as Firm as the Sabbath. Men who are placed in important positions, as those at the Health Retreat, are made the special objects of Satan's attacks. They are brought necessarily into the society of men and women. Some of these have a coarse, passionate, sensual nature, who when under temptation would do anything, regardless of God, regardless of consequences. They would break down the barriers of the marriage relation, that they may form new connections.

God gave only one cause why a wife should leave her husband, or the husband leave his wife, which was adultery. Let this ground be prayerfully considered. Marriage was from the creation constituted by God a divine ordinance. The marriage institution was made in Eden. The Sabbath of the fourth commandment was instituted in Eden, when the foundations of the world were laid, when the morning stars sang together, and all the sons of God shouted for joy. Then let this, God's institution of marriage, stand before you as firm as the Sabbath of the fourth commandment.

We inquire, What can be said or done to stop the moral declension that has been taking root in the Health Retreat? May God forgive those who have had the experience of years in connection with the cause and work of God, and yet will by practice bring in a state of things that will endanger virtue and modesty and self-respect of girls and women. I must urge upon you that which I know, from the light which God has been pleased to give me. I have been shown that men and women enjoying the religion of Jesus Christ will not be uneasy, restless, discontented, changeable; the peace of Christ in the heart will give solidity to character.

Sacredness of the Marriage Covenant. I was in the night season in my dreams brought in connection with the Health Retreat. I felt grieved to see you unhappy and much discouraged. . . . But while I was distressed over this revelation to me, there was One speaking with you, Dr. Q. His words reproved you, but were mingled with tender compassion. I cannot write the exact words as He spoke them. I will try my best to give you the import of them. He said:

"You are nourishing despondency, but in this you are not wise; you will become weak and inefficient. This will give the enemy advantage over you. God would have you grow nearer and closer to Himself, to resemble the image and character of Christ. Your heart is the seat of many tumultuous feelings, which you do not strive vigorously to overcome. You do not put your full heart and will into the work of cleansing the soul temple. Your mind is unwisely exercised on the subject of divorce from your wife. God is not leading you in this. You are not keeping this matter bound within your own mind. You are telling your ideas and plans to others, and in thus doing you are preparing the way for Satan to affect the minds of others by your suggestions.

"The matter of the marriage covenant does not stand sacred and elevated in your mind as it should, and you will be certainly in danger of pursuing a wrong course yourself, and endangering other souls by your suggestions. Your mind while stirred up on this subject cannot be prepared to do the best work, and you cannot be an earnest seeker for the blessing of the Lord, unless you shall come up on higher ground. You have done positive injury to the hearts and minds of others. Close quickly the door of your heart that has been open to the enemy. Open wide the door of your heart and invite Jesus to come in. You will then have a balance wheel to your somewhat erratic nature, that you can put your whole being into your work, realizing its importance. Improve every opportunity to work your way upward, exerting a firm and healthful influence. Lose no time in this matter. If you would be a free and happy man, you must resist the enemy.''. . .

The Thoughts on a Higher Channel. Dr. Q, your mind is not in a healthful state. You center your mind upon things that do not bring to you physical or mental soundness. You must have a change of heart; then your thoughts will flow into a higher, purer channel. You enjoy the society of women and girls. This becomes to you a snare. In such an institution the physician's mind should be constantly uplifted to God for strength and wisdom. There is constant danger of the thoughts taking a low level. Unless the Lord is the center of attraction, unless He is a special defense against the temptations of the enemy, he [Satan] will gain power over your mind and separate you from God.

Need of Heart Religion. In a dream on another occasion you were presented before me. Your head was bowed down upon a table. You were almost unconscious. Words were spoken to you with a firm, decided emphasis: ''Put that out of your hand! You need not take that; your life is not your own; your medicine is not needed to bring you peace and rest. What you need is heart religion, a heart purified, refined, elevated from common things, taking hold upon the divine. Be a man. Call your wife to your side, become better acquainted with the truth, be molded by the Spirit of God, and you will have peace. If you take the right course, if you are unwavering in the truth, if you keep your own soul in the love of God, you will be in the hands of the Lord the means of saving your wife, and in her turn, if she accepts the truth of heavenly origin, if she is a meek and humble follower of Christ, she will be the means in the hands of God of being a great blessing to you. . . .

Now, Dr. Q, stand up in your God-given manhood! Lift the cross of Christ daily, uplift your thoughts into a higher, purer channel. Respect your marriage vows, and be God's own servant for the uplifting of the human race. If you are an overcomer, you will be among those who will have possession of all things; the eternal weight of glory will be yours.

The Result of Undue Familiarity. There is an animal that strikes the arm with feebleness the moment it touches it. The muscles become as if paralyzed. In a similar way will it be with you spiritually, if your thoughts are allowed to run in a certain channel, and you give attention and preferences to young girls or married women. All this familiarity is death to spirituality.

Let your affections and your sympathies entwine about God, else your impulses will become impure, your character will be defective, your heart estranged from God. Whoever touched or handled that which pollutes, and yet continued pure? The soul cannot remain pure breathing the atmosphere of that which taints and corrupts. These things steal the heart away from God. The soul withers and becomes deformed, because the tent is pitched too near Sodom to breathe the pure atmosphere of heaven.

Our Only Safety. The violation of one of God's precepts does violence to your moral nature. For Christ's sake, I implore you to reach a higher standard. Give yourself unreservedly to the Lord. You have lessons to learn that your only safety is to meet the requirements of God, to present your body "a living sacrifice, holy, acceptable unto God, which is your reasonable service." Then the Word of God will be found a pleasant and profitable guide, a light to your feet, and a lamp to your path. Then you can bear perplexities, and they will not overcome you; for you know that your soul is riveted to the eternal Rock, because you abide by the simple truth of God.—Letter 8, 1888.

25. A Literature Evangelist

Counsel to a Woman Literature Evangelist. I have received two letters from you, and have a desire to relieve your mind if I can. Your position was a very remarkable one, and God gave me a decided message for you. I did not consider from the facts presented that your case was without hope; but your perception of what constituted right and wrong was so low in the scale that it was entirely unsafe for you to be traveling and be canvassing and giving Bible readings, and be exposed to temptations. [You are] one who could not distinguish in the Word of God what sin is, in giving your body to be polluted by a man, whatever may be his profession, and claim to be relieved [forgiven]. This matter was shown to me to be a heinous sin in the sight of God, and yet your senses were so benumbed and demoralized that you would continue to canvass for our religious books and give Bible readings, and you committing fornication.

Reproof From God. The law of God proclaimed upon Mount Sinai, "Thou shalt not commit adultery," and yet you who transgressed that law in so marked a manner were teaching others the Bible. God did not accept your labors. You ask if the Lord gave me that letter to give to you. I say

He did. The holy God of Israel will not serve with your sins. That message was given of God. If you have had, since that message was given, a new sense of what constitutes sin, if you have become truly converted, a child of God in place of being a transgressor of His law, there is no one who will be more pleased than myself. I could not present your sin before you in too strong language.

So Little Sense of Sin. I had presented before me several, living in different States, who were engaged in the canvassing work who were unfit to have any connection with the work of God. They would dishonor God, and bring the truth into reproach. They would make light of sin. They were dishonoring their own bodies. But not one among the number was having so little sense of what sin was, as you. Anyone pursuing the course you did, and belied apparently to the criminality and degradation of such a course, was just terrible. You had not a sense of the aggravated character of sin.

God's Patience With Sinners. The message was given Jonah to Nineveh, that in forty days it should be destroyed. Nineveh repented, and God spared the wicked city, because kings and nobles humbled themselves greatly before God, and the Lord gave Nineveh chance for repentance. If the Lord in His great mercy treats your case in a similar manner, oh, I shall be so thankful. If He grants you probation in which to manifest that repentance that needeth not to be repented of, because you see and sense the real nature of sin, that you abhor yourself because of your sin, and have an abhorrence likewise of the sin, the Lord is gracious, of pitying tenderness and loving kindness. "If we confess our sins, He is faithful and just to forgive us our sins, and to cleanse us from all unrighteousness" [1 John 1:9].

I believe you have confessed your sin, and that God will pardon the sin as He has promised. The only drawback in my mind is that the very same want of perception of what constituted sin, in the prostituting of your body, giving it up to the use of an adulterer, a whoremonger, and you connected with the work and cause of God giving Bible readings, as though the Lord would serve with your sins while you were engaged in His work and voluntarily seeking the embrace of an adulterer [is still a weakness with you].

Divine Mercy to the City of Nineveh. I presented you with the matter as presented to me, and tell you that God abhors all such things. If your moral sensibilities are quickened, it is through the converting power of God. If you are transformed in character, the Lord knows all about that. And if you have through repentance been uplifted to reach a high and holy standard, I cannot myself say the Lord will not regard your case in the same light He regarded Nineveh.

Said the king of Nineveh, "Let man and beast be covered with sackcloth, and cry mightily unto God: yea, let them turn every one from his evil way, and from the violence that is in their hands. Who can tell if God will turn and repent, and turn away from His fierce anger, that we perish not? And God saw their works, that they turned from their evil way; and God repented of the evil, that He had said that He would do unto them; and He did it not" [Jonah 3:8-10]. Read this over carefully, and if the Lord [should] trust you with His work, I have not a word of objection. This is all I can say to you.

Now, please take your case to the Lord, and if you are in communion with Him, He will hear your prayers, and will guide you in judgment. My heart pities you. The first time the sin was committed, it was done without so much time for meditation; the second sins were committed after time to meditate, after time to consider the matter in the light of the Word of God, in the face of the seventh commandment.

That you should voluntarily submit your body to the man who led you astray, and you engaged in seeking to enlighten other minds in regard to the commandments, is a most decided exhibition of depravity, and reveals a character as presented to me untrustworthy, and you were incapable of discerning why you should not go right on with the work as you had done.

Public Confession Not Always Best. But I leave the matter where it is. I could say to you to go to trustworthy persons in the conference (not men, but women), and talk with them; but I am inclined to think that should you do this you would be giving publicity to those things which would cause all to be removed from you; and they would not encourage you or accept you to engage in any branch of the work, when they should understand the matter as it is. I must now leave this matter between you and your God, and please do not trouble me anymore with it. I have no disposition to expose you, but leave you to develop character. I pity you and hope that you will move in discretion, and become altogether that which God would have you.—Letter 95, 1893.

26. A Public Evangelist*

Strong to Move Crowds, Weak to Manage Self. You will see before this reaches you that the Lord has again visited

---

*The evangelist to whom these letters were written sometimes conducted several series of meetings in one area, then moved away to the next while his wife remained to carry on with the interest and follow up with Bible studies. This situation was far from ideal. He finally fell into the sin of adultery and even rejected the Spirit of Prophecy and the counsel of the General Conference leaders. The Review and Herald announced that his credentials were revoked. A few years before his death he repented and returned to the Lord.

His people by giving me a testimony. In this view I was shown that you were not standing in the clear light and you are in danger of bringing a reproach upon the cause of God by moving as you happen to feel. It is Satan's intent to destroy you. He is seeking to keep your mind in a constant state of agitation, stirring it up that it may cast up mire and dirt instead of the peaceful fruits of righteousness. . . .

But, Brother R, I was shown that you now should be very circumspect in your deportment and in your words. You are watched by enemies. You have great weaknesses for a man who is as strong as you are to move the crowd. As you are now separated from your wife there will be suspicion and jealousy, and falsehoods will be framed [even] if you give no occasion. But if you are not cautious, you will bring a reproach upon the cause of God which could not soon be wiped away. You may feel, as I saw you had felt, that if you were not going to live with your wife, you wished to be free from her. You are restless, uneasy, and unsettled. Satan is tempting you to make a foolish man of yourself. Now is the time for you to show yourself a man, to exhibit the grace of God by your patience, your fortitude, and courage. . . .

Danger in Confidants. You need to consecrate yourself to God, and not dwell upon your troubles. Be careful how you are enticed to make women your confidants or to allow them to make you their confidant. Keep aloof from the society of women as much as you can. You will be in danger. Remember, we are living amid the perils of the last days. Almost everything is rotten and corrupt.

Look to God, pray, oh, pray, as you never have before to be kept by the power of God through faith. In God you can stand untainted, without a stain or blemish. Fasten your hold upon God. Look to Him in faith that you may be a par-

taker of the divine nature, having escaped the corruption
that is in the world through lust. God will bring you off vic-
torious if you will live a humble life of prayer and dependent trust.—Letter 23, 1871.

No Relish for God's Word. In the last vision given me
your case was presented before me. I have been waiting to
see if you had a tender, sensitive, or a seared, conscience. I
have had the following written out for a long time but have
thought I would wait till you made some move yourself. I
was shown that you have not lived up to the light. You have
departed far from the light. The Lord has been following you
with reproofs and counsel to preserve you from ruining your
own soul and bringing a reproach upon His cause. I was
shown that you have been retrograding rather than advancing
and growing in grace and the knowledge of truth. . . .

You have made girls and women the theme of thought,
rather than the Word of God. Your mind has been restless
and dissatisfied if it could not be occupied with girls and
women. You could not relish the study of the Word of God
while your thoughts have been upon subjects which war
against the soul. There is no excuse for your life of folly.

A Double-minded Minister. From what has been shown
me you are a transgressor of the seventh commandment.
How then can your mind be in harmony with the precious
Word of God, truths which cut you at every turn? If you had
been betrayed into this folly unwittingly, it would be more
excusable, but you have not. You have been warned. You
have been reproved and counseled. You have apparently
received the reproof, but not in heart sufficient to die to the
carnal mind. You have not set to work to eradicate the evil.
You have soon lost the smart of the chastening rod of the
Lord, and rushed on in as great foolishness as ever, like a

fool to the correction of stocks. Your love for self-indulgence has become a warring lust.

You love the society of girls and women. During a series of meetings you have allowed your mind to plan and contrive how you can get into the society of young girls or women and not betray your true feelings. You will run into temptation when you have not moral power to resist temptation. Your mind is constantly impure because the fountain is never cleansed. You have found no delight in diligent, careful searching of the Scriptures. . . .

Unchastity of Thought and Action. God has erected the barriers of testimonies as a wall about you to guard you from falling under the specious wiles of the enemy, but you break all these down and press over everything to follow your inclination. Your sorrow for your sins is like that of those who anciently rent their garments to express their grief but did not afflict their souls. You have not a correct sense of what sin is. The aggravating character of unchastity of thought and actions you have not sensed. Your mind is carnal, and that almost continually. If you really were sorry for your sins, if you really had a true sense of your wrongs, you would exercise that repentance that needeth not to be repented of.

More Harm Than Help to the Cause. I desire now to state facts. I have been shown that your life and your labors in the cause of God for some years have been a greater injury to the precious cause of present truth than a benefit. Had you had no part in this work and been separated entirely from it, you would have saved much heart sorrow to those who love the cause of God; and you would have saved them much hard labor which has been forced upon them to counteract your wrong influence.

The labor that has been required to get you right and to

keep you from disgracing the cause, had it been spent on converting souls from error to truth —and had the laborers had nothing whatever to do in regard to you—the interest and strength of the cause of present truth would stand better today in California as well as in the East.

Influence of an Erring Minister. Satan has made you his agent to carry out his mind. The great stir and great excitement you have made in discussions from time to time, and the apparent success you have had, has built you up in your own self-righteousness. Allowing you to labor as you have been permitted to labor when your heart was not right with God, has done you great injury. You have not searched your own heart and afflicted your soul before God. You have felt too lightly your terrible mistakes in the past. Everything has been done to save you from utter disgrace and ruin. You have been patiently borne with, and when wholly unfit for the sacred work, in order to save your soul you have been permitted to continue your labors while hearts have groaned and ached under the burden of your foolish, sinful course.

Had you been left to yourself long ago, till you gave the evidence that God was indeed with you and that you were a thoroughly reformed man, you might now be of some use in this solemn work. But I saw that we were risking altogether too much in encouraging you to go out to labor to convert sinners to Christ when your way has been polluted before God, your heart all stained with sins. The true servants of God are judged to be like yourself. No longer should you mar the work of God with your corrupt, your carnal, heart, and thus miserably represent the cause of present truth.

Some Success No Evidence of God's Acceptance. In order for you to do good you must live a new life that is in harmony with God. Your perverse nature has not been transformed. You are not at peace with God or with yourself. You are in bondage to the great adversary of souls, in subjection to the old man of sin. You are not a free man in Christ. There is needed a spiritual change in you before God can work with you. You may argue that you have success as you labor. So do many who are at war with God have a measure of success. If some do embrace the truth while the arguments you use are so convincing, it is no evidence you are in a state of even acceptance with God. . . .

A Life of Known Mental Sin. If it had only stopped there—but it did not. You felt for a little time the evil of your course, but not as fully as you should, how you had been deceived by Satan, infatuated; and your eyes never did have the mist fully removed from them. You humbled your heart before God, and He accepted your humiliation. You soon became careless again, and allowed your mind to become filled again with vain and impure imaginings. You were a little more cautious, but full of deception. Your mind was active to invent means to gain your object. . . .

The power of great passion has been your apology for vice. Your life has been a shame—nothing in it of which you might glory. You have had great depression if you were not strained up to some excitement and not had some girl or woman to attract you and to listen to your troubles in regard to your wife. Shame, shame should cover you for your course.—Letter 52, 1876.

Daily Conversion for a Sacred Work. God has shown me your case so fully I dare not let you go on in deception as to your true condition. I greatly fear that you will fail of everlasting life, that after you have preached to others upon the binding claims of God's law you will fail to carry out in your own life the holy principles of the law of God, and will make shipwreck of faith.

You are so much swallowed up in yourself that unless you are consecrated to God and have a living daily faith in God and obtain His grace and power, you will be a hindrance to the advancement of the truth. I cannot see the cause of God marred and suffer through your inefficiency or through your blind mistakes. You must be a daily converted man or you are unfit for the sacred work in which you are engaged. I know more of your peculiar temperament and your dangers than others can.

Appeal to Women for Sympathy. Your trouble with the sisters has come in consequence of your drawing upon their sympathies. You relate your trials and enlist their pity for you whom they think a great sufferer. You then yield to your feelings, put on an appearance as though you were enduring almost martyrdom. You lead them out to give you care and attention which is not really proper, and bring yourself in a position where you are easily tempted. You should have learned by your trials in the past to shun anything which has the least appearance of familiarity with the sisters, married or unmarried. Let your affections center upon God. Rely upon Him for support rather than on human sympathy.

You are very weak in this direction, but the cause of God must not be marred with your weakness and indiscretion. This is your danger, and you are overcome, and then a wound is brought upon the cause of God that can never be fully healed.—Letter 53, 1876.

Attitude of the Evangelist After Loss of His Credentials. Dear Sir: I have been troubled exceedingly in regard to your case, and yet have not known what to say to you. I was very reluctant to say a word to discourage you, for I know what terrible sadness discouragement brings to the soul. I thought when your credentials were not renewed you would quietly settle down and be willing to be retired, that you would know if it was among the possibilities consistent with reason and religion in the great need we are of laborers, you would have received credentials. I could not use my influence in favor of this.

In the last vision given me, the great white throne was presented before me, with the Judge of all the earth to pass sentence upon the congregated multitude. The ledger of heaven was opened, and those about the throne were judged according to the deeds done in the body.

Your name was registered as weighed in the balance and found wanting. Your name was registered as a transgressor of the commandments of God.

Opportunity to Redeem the Past. God in His great mercy gave you opportunity to redeem the past. When you had shown repentance He pitied you. . . . You were placed in a good field of labor, and had you conducted yourself as a Christian should, you might then have had that repentance that needeth not to be repented of.

You were, for a time, humble and thankful, but your heart had so long been given up to perversity and to self-indulgence, that you could not see and sense your past course as so very offensive to God. Like Peter, you had been faithfully warned of your danger and of your defection of character; but you were self-confident and became jealous and acted like a spoiled child. . . .

God's Rejection of Ministerial Labor. After God had borne so long with your perversity, while you were professing to be a shepherd of the flock, you were granted another trial in answer to our sorrowful petitions in your behalf. The Lord opened the way before you. We felt very sad for you; and when we saw how the matter resulted, we felt worse than before.

I was shown that your labors as a minister would be no longer accepted of God. Your moral sense is in no way strengthened by your last test and trial. You did not take and keep the position of a penitent man, humbling yourself daily before God, under a sense of His great mercy and your sinfulness. God does not connect with you.

Contrition and prayer should have been your attitude; and if you had preserved this penitential position you would not be where you now are, unfit to be entrusted with the solemn work of laboring for souls, jealous, surmising evil, selfish, and uncourteous. You and your wife are an offense to God. It was your privilege to place yourselves where God could have worked through you, but you did not do this. You had not a love for the study of the Word. You had no love for prayer.

David's Hour of Adversity. You did not take a humble position, as did David in view of his sin. After the commission of that great crime of his life, his entire character deteriorated. That crime recoiled terribly upon him. He was bearing a conscious sense of guilt. He felt that he had forfeited the love and loyalty of his subjects. He was weakened physically and morally. He lost his own self-respect and self-confidence. He scarcely dared trust his old and formerly tried advisers. Humbled and mournful was the procession that took that precipitate flight from his throne across the mount.

But David was never more worthy of admiration than in his hour of adversity. Never was this cedar of God truly greater than when wrestling with the storm and tempest. He was a man of the keenest temperament, which might have been raised to the strongest feelings of resentment. He was cut to the quick with the imputation of unmerited wrong. Reproach, he tells us, had broken his heart.

And it would not have been surprising if, stung to madness, he had given vent to his feelings of uncontrollable irritation, to bursts of vehement rage, and expressions of revenge. But there was nothing of this which would naturally be expected of a man with his stamp of character. With spirit broken and in tearful emotion, but without one expression of repining, he turns his back upon the scenes of his glory and also of his crime, and pursues his flight for his life.

Shimei comes forth as David passes and, with a storm of curses, hurls against him invectives, throwing stones and dirt. Said one of David's faithful men, "Let me go over, I pray thee, and take off his head." David in his sorrow and humility says, "Let him curse, because the Lord hath said unto him, Curse David. . . . Behold, my son, which came forth of my bowels, seeketh my life" (2 Sam. 16:9-11).

David's Refusal to Avenge Himself. In David is seen the saint of God. His fine and deep sense of feeling is not blunted. He senses his sin most keenly. . . .

The faithful Nathan had pronounced the judgment of God. The sword was never to leave his [David's] house; that which he had sown he was also to reap. He had often had a gloomy presentiment of the present hour. He had long wondered why the merited judgment was so long delayed. The God he had offended by bringing so great sin upon Israel as their leader, was now showing him that He is not a God that will lie, and that by terrible things in righteousness would He show His hatred of sin. He did indeed realize, "Be sure your sin will find you out."

But David showed the fine gold of his character under adversity and while suffering the retributive justice of God, in refusing to be avenged on Shimei, and in refusing to stoop to strategy or the arts of base expediency to gain his honor and his kingdom. . . .

He recalled how ofttimes God had worked for him, and thought, ''If He accepts my repentance He may yet give me His favor and turn my mourning to joy. He may remove my sackcloth and give me the garment of goodness. On the other hand, if He has no delight in me, if He has forgotten me, if He will leave me to exile or to perish, I will not murmur. I deserve His judgments and will submit to it all. I will bear the indignation of the Lord, because I have sinned against Him, until He plead my cause and execute judgment for me.''

Oh, what a wonderful change for David! From his throne and kingdom he is fleeing into a barren dry land with no water.

A Contrast With David's Case. I bring before you this lesson that you may see the contrast between your course under the reproof and displeasure of God and the course pursued by David. You have ever been ready to charge your discomfiture to somebody prejudiced against you. Instead of seeing that no one can have too strong feelings against a man professing to be a shepherd of the flock, who will corrupt the minds of the unsuspecting, you act as though you were a martyr suffering unjustly—a persecuted man who deserves the sympathy of the people. You have not a proper sense of sin. You are not right before God in motive or spirit. . . .

Confession, But No Real Penitence. After you changed your location to Texas and had shown by confessing some things that you were sorry for your sins, your course was not what the course of a penitent man should be. You felt aggrieved that you were assailed and your name reproached. You sympathized with yourself in this matter, and then settled back in a state of helpless backsliding. Your example and your influence were not those of a penitent man.

Meanwhile we felt sad indeed on your account and that

of your wife. Both of you have had great light and great privileges, and both gave yourselves into the enemy's hands while in the midst of light and opportunities and privileges. But we felt deep sorrow for you. We placed ourselves in your place and made the case our own. To have once taken an active part in the cause and then be set aside, having no part in it, seemed so terrible. We thought you had repented. We prayed for you very earnestly, and in a dream your case was presented before me.

A Second Trial, Although Unworthy. I dreamed that although you were wholly unworthy, God would give you another trial. At once we made what efforts we could to get you to Colorado. We knew we were doing this in direct opposition to leading brethren who knew your case. We took the responsibility upon ourselves. We told you this. When the vision was given me two years ago, some things were shown me in regard to your dangers, which I faithfully wrote to you, informing you what course you must pursue.

At the same time I pled most earnestly with you not to make a failure this time, that now was your time, now your day of opportunity; if you failed here it would be disastrous to you. I wrote private letters, I urged upon you what you must do and the earnest efforts you must put forth. Read Testimony No. 28. [See 3T 306-383.]

An Unheeded Warning. When in Colorado one year ago, your course grieved me, not from any personal difference, but I saw that you were not doing as God had told you you must do. My heart sank within me. I gave you a warning, but you did not heed it. I knew then, as I know now, that you were making a failure. I had your course marked out plainly in regard to the fruit we should see in you, if you would sense your state and improve this last trial. . . .

Character Demoralization by Vanity and Envy. When you went to Colorado you had an excellent field, an excellent home; and oh, so much better privileges than some of our brethren have. You were familiar with the truth which you presented to the people, and some responded to it. You were humble at first. . . . You continued to labor, but you began to think that you were really quite an acquisition to the cause, and resented everything that did not look as though your efforts were appreciated. Very early you began to complain and express your dissatisfaction. . . .

When we tried to set things in order, you were not one to humble yourself as did David. Contrast your feelings and your sense of sin with his repentance and humiliation. Your influence was on the side of the enemy. You were as a man in a maze. You began to recount what great good you had done, to reckon up those who had embraced the truth since you came to Colorado, when had it not been for publications and other influences aside from yours, there would have been but very few that would have balanced on the side of truth as your sheaves. You claim too much. . . .

There will be those who will solicit you to labor among them, and you may in your unsanctified heart flatter yourself that this is in your favor, and that you are of value. But do you suppose for a moment, if they could read your heart or have opened before them your past course of wickedness, they would be eager for your labors? It is because they have not a knowledge of your course and what long forbearance the people of God have exercised toward you. They know not how aggravating has been your case, how many testimonies of warning have been given you, all of which have been unheeded. Should they know the matters as they are, they would give no encouragement to your preaching. . . .

David's Well-learned Lessons. The fruits of repentance are seen in the example of David. He learned the lesson of resignation under affliction, patience under injuries, and of humble, childlike reliance upon God. In your discouraged, dark condition, you should have both commenced as young converts, seeking to have no will nor way of your own, no surmising nor judging of the motives of others, and leaving forever the long, fretting, complaining years of the past. Many who see not as God seeth, but view matters from man's standpoint, might reason that with David there might have been excuse for repining, and that the sincerity of his repentance years before might have excepted him from present judgment.

David might have thought so himself. He might have said, I have for a long time been obedient, and this should offset against my disobedience. It is hard for me in my old age to meet this sweeping blast. My life generally has been a life of faithful discharge of duty as God's honored servant, the king of Israel, the singer of His church. It is hard now to hang my harp upon the willow and remain tuneless and become a wandering exile. "My own son seeketh my life."

Excuses for Sin of No Value With God. But David makes no excuse. Justice points to the broken tablets of the broken law and draws her sword against the transgressor. All apologies or excuses for sin are of no value with God. The sentiment of the soul of David was, Who shall testify to lessen the guilt of the sinner when God testifies against him? God's verdict—guilty—has gone forth, and man cannot erase it. [David knows the Scripture]: "Cursed is every one that continueth not in all things which are written in the book of the law to do them." David utters no complaint. The most eloquent psalm he ever sang was when he was climbing Mount Olivet, weeping and barefooted, yet humbled in spirit, unselfish and generous, submissive and resigned.

The royal fugitive does not render evil for evil or railing for railing. He does not harbor revengeful feelings in his heart, but amid his own woes he is kind, noble, and sympathetic. Oh, what a marked contrast has been your course. . . .

Law of Sowing and Reaping. You have had every opportunity, every privilege, every advantage, but you have not improved them. When you came to Colorado, if you had both sought God like young converts, studied your Bibles, walked humbly with God, prayed earnestly, and watched thereunto, you would have shown that you prized the boon of eternal life.

But you would not appreciate heaven. Although you have, on account of your sins, been most terribly threatened of God and warned for years of His punishment which is sure to come for transgression, yet all the time you have been grieving the Saviour. He has made you the object of His unwearied love and tender solicitude. He and all heaven have been ashamed of you and looked upon your course with loathing.

When the husbandman sows corn, he reaps corn. If he sows wheat, he reaps wheat. If he sows poisonous seeds, he will have the same to harvest. Thus with yourself as a responsible agent. If you sow to the flesh, you will of the flesh reap corruption. If you sow licentiousness, you will reap that which you have sown. The seed sown produces its kind. . . .

Possible Accomplishment of a Second Trial. God gave you another trial. Oh, that you could have appreciated it, and offered earnest, heartfelt prayer with true penitence and living faith to grasp the precious promise. Had you with willing heart practiced self-denial, resisted temptation, there would have been increased strength with every effort to overcome self. Every new achievement of principle will smooth the way for achievements of the same kind, the fruit of every moral victory. This victory is the seed sown which produces its kind, placing the sower on higher ground for every triumph of righteousness gained. Every virtuous action strengthens the spiritual sinews for new virtue, and every vice repeated rivets the fetters of vice. There is a growing strength in habit, and by it every action makes way for repetition. . . .

Retired Life After Loss of Credentials. If you can save your own soul by a humble, penitent life, that is the greatest work you can do. God is merciful, but you should not attempt to teach others. You have lost the power of God to teach. Your work is not acceptable to God.

It is alarming how rapidly the sin of licentiousness is coming in among us. While writing out these individual, personal testimonies, your case was urged upon me with great power in the night season; and I cannot forbear writing to you. My soul is burdened day and night for the Israel of God. . . .

Loss of the Power of God. I hoped that you would be of sufficient understanding to know when no credentials were given you that you should keep humbled and retired. You might have known that it was my words that had to be spoken in answer to questions put directly, that settled the matter in regard to your receiving credentials.

But when I see your reports in the paper my heart is sad. No such reports should enter the columns of our paper. How do those whom you have sought to ruin look upon these reports? How do those in _____ regard them? It is because the fine perception is dimmed in those in charge of the paper that any of your reports find access to its columns. The high standard of truth and purity is lowered. Your spirit of independence and self-esteem shown since the conference at Battle Creek is anything but the spirit you would have could you discern yourself and have a true sense of sin.—Letter 6, 1880.

27. An Honored Minister

Loss of Influence and Reputation. Dear Brother H: I have somewhat to say unto thee. . . .

My brother, you have had the respect of the church, old and young. But your course is condemned of God, and you have not had His Spirit, and you are not a free man. You have pursued a course that has caused your good to be evil spoken of. The very things that transpired at the Piedmont Sabbath school reunion, I would not have [had] occur for thousands of dollars. You, a gray-haired man, lying at full length with your head in the lap of Georgie S. Had I done my duty, I would have rebuked you there. Many saw this and made remarks about it. After such exhibitions as this, of what value would be your admonitions to them to be guarded against everything of this free and easy familiarity? You have yourself neutralized your efforts to elevate the young by your example.

The course of intimacy with Sister S and her family has been a subject of remark. And how could you expect to have influence with the young as a father when such manifest want of judgment and such weakness has been exhibited by you? If you will only be a man in your old age instead of a sentimental lover; if you would only be guarded, God would not remove His wisdom from you as He has done. Your reputation would have been dearer to you than your very life. Better, far better, go down to the grave with honor untarnished, than to live with a reproach upon your name.

When the Lord Is Not Supreme. Now look, my brother, at the years you have been living in unlawful sympathy and love with another man's wife. And you have a daughter who would be glad to give you attention and sympathy and make a home for you, but you have been so completely infatuated that everything in this life that was sensible and proper has been distasteful and insipid to you. I do not feel that the charm is broken, that you are a free man. You have not broken the snare. The Lord is not supreme with you.

Now, my brother, it would be folly for you to think that you have wisdom to discern spiritual things while you have been growing weaker and weaker for years in moral power, and separating from the God of wisdom. The letters written to your wife are harsh and unfeeling. The withdrawing of your support in a large degree is not wisdom or right on your part. And had she not a cause when she was at Oakland to be jealous of you? Did not she see in you the interest, sympathy, and love you gave to Sister S?

Now, for Christ's sake, save your harsh condemnation of others, for this shows that you are not Christlike, that you have another spirit. I write thus plainly because I feel deeply that you need to make a more determined effort than you have done before you stand free in the sight of God. All your sharpness and overbearing comes from you with an ill grace. Do humble yourself under the hand of God. Do make sure of the favor of God, and put sin away from you.

There are but few who know to what extent this intimacy has gone, and God forbid it shall be known and your influence lost to God's cause and your soul lost. I beg of you not to take it upon you to pronounce judgment against anyone but yourself.—Letter 10, 1885.

For the Good of the Cause. Dear Brother Butler: . . . I have spoken quite freely upon some things. I thought I had to do this. Am inclined to say I will hold my peace henceforth, but as I am not my own and as I am mightily wrought upon at times to write, I dare not say this. I have but one object in view—not only the present but future good of the cause and work of God. Should I resist these impressions to write, when I am so burdened? I cannot now promise. I must ponder these things in my heart. I must pray about them, and obey the movings of the Spirit of God or withdraw myself from having any connection with the work.

The Lord knows I am not pleased with this kind of work. I love and respect my brethren, and would not in the slightest manner demerit them, cause them pain; but I have tried to move with an eye single to the glory of God. I feel a sadness now upon me and confusion that I cannot see clearly my duty.

God's Answer to Prayer for Victory. I wrote some things to H. He wrote me that it was just as I had stated the matter. I was so burdened with a dream I had that I arose at three o'clock and wrote to Elder H that he had not kept his promise, that while he was engaged in teaching the commandments of God he was breaking them, that he was giving attentions to Sister S which should be bestowed only upon his wife. I wrote very pointedly to him.

He admitted my statements, said he had prayed over the matter and felt that his course was wrong, but did not say he would cease this thing forever. He says,

"Your strong condemnation of me is only just. That I know, and feel the difficulty with me was this:

it was so hard for me to realize the sinfulness of my course. My reason, my judgment, the testimony and the Scriptures, all combined to teach me that it was wrong. Yet it had such a hold of me that I failed to realize it as I should. I could not bring myself to feel the extent of my wrong, and gradually it proved a snare to me. But I had been making it a subject of special prayer some time before I received your last letter, that God would enable me to see it in its proper light and to feel over it as I should; and I have reason to believe that my prayer was answered.

"If I know anything of the blessing of grace, I know that I was blessed in the effort. I greatly needed this blessing to enable me to do the work aright, which was put upon me here. It was expressed of all that I was helped of heaven to write the report on the matter of the arrest of our people for working on the Sunday and other important writings which it fell to me to do. But I am painfully conscious of my weakness and that my only safety is in constant watchfulness such as I did not exercise before. I see now that it is a question of life and death with me and shall strive to act accordingly."—Letter 73, 1886.

Workings of an Unsanctified Heart. Dear Brother Butler.* I am troubled in regard to Elder H. He writes me nothing, and I feel deeply pained on his account. It seems sometimes to me that the Lord is testing us to see whether we will deal faithfully in regard to sin in one of our honored men. The time is close at hand when the General Con-

---

*This letter was sent to Elder George I. Butler, the General Conference president, but Ellen White also directly addresses Elder H, the guilty minister.

ference will have to decide the points whether or not to renew his credentials.

If the Conference does this, they will be saying virtually, "We have confidence in you as a man whom God recognizes as His messenger; one to whom He has entrusted the sacred responsibilities of caring for the sheep of the Lord's pasture; one who will be in all things a faithful shepherd, a representative of Christ." But can we do this? Have we not seen the workings of an unsanctified heart?

A Man Bewitched. The persistency in Elder H to accept and claim Mrs. S as his—what shall I call it—his affinity? What is this? Who can name it? Is Elder H one who has hated the light God has given him, showing that his preferences for Mrs. S's society, and his intimacy with her, was sinful as in the light of the Word of God? Or did he accept the message and act upon it?

Notwithstanding, I went to Elder H with the testimony given me of God, yet he did not reform. His course has said, "I will do as I please in the matter; there is no sin in it." He promised before God what he would do, but he broke his promises made to Brother C. H. Jones, W. C. White, and myself, and his feelings did not decidedly change; but he seems to act like a man bewitched, under the spell of the devil, who had no power over his own inclinations. Notwithstanding all the light given, he has evidenced no real conviction or sense of sin; no repentance, no reformation. Hearts have ached sorely over this state of things, but they had no power to change his heart or his purposes.

Perversion of God-given Powers. Now, we should be very grateful for the help of Elder H in England, and in Switzerland, but what can we decide upon? We must have evidence that he is clear before God. We do not want to make a light matter of sin, and say to the sinner, "It shall be well with thee." We do not want to connect Elder H with the work here unless he has a connection with God. We do not want to have the drawback that would come by connecting a man with the work who has a blot on his garments. We cannot pass lightly over this matter.

The plague of sin is upon Elder H, and pain and sorrow are upon the souls of all who are aware of this chapter in his experience. Christ is dishonored. A man blessed with superior light and knowledge, endowed with great capacity for good, that he may by a life of obedience and fidelity to God become equal with angels [and] his life measure with the life of God, has perverted his God-given powers to administer to lust, coveting the wife of another. God finds Elder H setting at naught the most costly lessons of experience, violating the most solemn admonitions of God, that he may continue in sin.

I have hoped and prayed that he would restore reason to its right throne and break the fetters that for years Satan has been weaving about him, soul and body, and that the clouds that have shadowed his pathway be removed, and Christ come to his soul to revive and bless it. Christ will lift the heavy burden from weary shoulders, and give rest and peace to those who will wear His yoke and lift His burdens.

Appeal to a Leading Worker. I will say, Elder H, What can be the character of your experience when in the face of many warnings and reproofs you continue to pursue a course condemned of God? Can you think well of yourself? Just think of Jesus, crowned with thorns and nailed to the cross for our sins, and let it humble—yes, let it break—your heart. Look at the meekness of Christ, His loveliness, and then bow in the dust with shame and humiliation.

Will you please think what you would do in case one of our leading men should be found in the position you are in?

Could you, without any greater evidence on his part of the sense of his sin than you have given, advise that he have credentials as one of pure and holy purposes before God? Cannot you see you are placing your fellow laborers in a very unpleasant and unenviable position? Will they venture to become responsible for your character and your influence in the future in the work and cause of God?

Responsibility of Greater Light. Your case has been shown me to be worse than that of Elder R, because you had greater light, capacity, and influence; and his course is a beacon to warn you off from following in his steps. Elder R's credentials were taken away from him; he is a deeply repentant man, humbled in the dust.

Supposing David should, after being reproved by Nathan, have repeated the same offense, would the Lord then have had compassion upon him? But he repented bitterly; he declared his transgression was ever before him. Hear his humiliating confession, and listen to his despairing cries.

Cleansing of the Camp. We must as a people arouse and cleanse the camp of Israel. Licentiousness, unlawful intimacy, and unholy practices are coming in among us in a large degree; and ministers who are handling sacred things are guilty of sin in this respect. They are coveting their neighbors' wives, and the seventh commandment is broken. We are in danger of becoming a sister to fallen Babylon, of allowing our churches to become corrupted, and filled with every foul spirit, a cage for every unclean and hateful bird; and will we be clear unless we make decided movements to cure the existing evil?

Will you have others follow your example? Will you wish them to pass over the ground you have traveled, and feel that they have done no great wrong? Without repentance and conversion, you are a ruined man.

I hear you [Elder H] are taking treatment at the sanitarium, acting as chaplain, speaking in the Tabernacle. Now, this does not look right for you to take such positions, until you have done all in your power to correct past evils.

Self-righteousness and Inward Corruption. I have felt, for your sake, restrained from opening the matter of Mrs. S's infidelity to her husband, but I fear I have neglected my duty. If we had dealt with this matter as if it had been the case of a lay member of the church, I believe God would have then sent you repentance that needed not to be repented of.

Our pity, our love, to save you from reproach, has hurt you. My heart is so sad and agonized at times for you, I can only weep. I say, "Must he be lost? Must he, after suffering for the truth's sake, after standing in its defense until he is old and gray-headed, become an idolater, as did Solomon? Will he, for the love of a woman, trample down the law of God and look about him as much as to say, I do no sin; I am all right?"

Need of Heart Change, Not Change of Location. Will we be clear to let such things be concealed and sins hidden, with no real evidence of repentance or reform? Your leaving California does not give you a new heart. You are out of sight of the infatuating influence of your "adorable charmer," but this does not change the affections or impulses of the heart. Elder W might have finished his course with joy had it not been for sensual practices, but he was led away of his own lusts and enticed. The days and years which might have been his very best were his worst.

We see in the character of Solomon intellectual greatness combined with moral degradation. He might have gone forward from strength to strength, but instead of this he went backward from weakness to weakness. After a life of promise, his history was one of deterioration.

The Very Brink of the Precipice. My brother, my heart yearns toward you for Christ's sake. You have been attempting what other ministers have attempted—to harmonize light with darkness, Christ with Belial, purity with impurity, good with evil. The result will be moral ruin, unless you can be aroused to see that you are standing upon the very brink of the precipice. There are many such cases that I have to write about.

It alarms me to see how the sin of licentiousness is coming in upon us. I felt this when I wrote to Elder Butler upon this point at the last General Conference, begging him to do all that he could to fence against what was coming in upon us. We must elevate the standard and build up barriers about the soul so that nothing shall mar its simplicity and purity, and thus defile the religious character. God has given man intellect, and let every soul beware how this great gift is prostituted to the soul's eternal ruin.

Repentance and Rebaptism. There is no more hope of you than of any common sinner, nor as much, unless you greatly humble your soul before God, repent, and are converted. Take the first steps in the way to life—repentance, faith, and baptism. You have tampered with the divine safeguards of your peace. If you refuse to listen to the voice of reproof, if you choose your own course, if you will not allow the grace of Christ to transform you, your guilt will be as much greater than that of the common sinner as your advantages of light and influence have been greater.

Great care should be exercised in companionship and friendship lest the soul be imperiled, lest there be even an appearance of evil which in the eyes of others would lower the standard of religious principle and sap the foundation of religious belief.

The Sad Example of Solomon. How many, even in the ranks of Sabbathkeepers, are forming unsanctified connections. Men who have wives, and women who have husbands, are showing affection and giving undue attention to [those of the opposite sex]. How many men of promise there are in our ranks who no longer have pure faith and holy trust in God, because they have betrayed sacred trusts. Noble aspirations are quenched. Their steps are retrograding because they covet another man's wife or are unduly familiar with unmarried women. Their frivolous conduct leads them to break the seventh commandment.

Of Solomon, the inspired record says, "His wives turned away his heart after other gods: and his heart was not perfect with the Lord his God" (1 Kings 11:4).

Perpetuating Power of Evil Influence. This is no theme to be treated with a smile. The heart that loves Jesus will not desire the unlawful affections of another. Every want is supplied in Christ. This superficial affection is of the same character as that exalted enjoyment which Satan promised Eve. It is coveting that which God has forbidden.

When it is too late, hundreds can warn others not to venture upon the precipice. Intellect, position, wealth can never, never take the place of moral qualities. The Lord esteems clean hands, a pure heart, and noble, earnest devotion to God and the truth above the golden wedge of Ophir. An evil influence has a perpetuating power. I wish I could set this matter before God's commandment-keeping people just as it has been shown me. Let the sad memory of Solomon's apostasy warn every soul to shun the same precipice. His weakness and sin are handed down from generation to generation.

The greatest king that ever wielded a scepter, of whom it

had been said that he was the beloved of God, through
misplaced affection became contaminated and was miserably forsaken of his God. The mightiest ruler of the earth
had failed to rule his own passions. Solomon may have
been saved ''as by fire,'' yet his repentance could not ef-
face those high places, nor demolish those stones, which
remained as evidences of his crimes. He dishonored God,
choosing rather to be controlled by lust than to be a partaker
of the divine nature.

What a legacy Solomon's life has committed to those
who would use his example to cover their own base ac-
tions! We must either transmit a heritage of good or evil.
Shall our lives and our example be a blessing or a curse?
Shall people look at our graves and say, He ruined me, or,
He saved me? . . .

Ministers Subjects of Satan's Temptations. Satan's special efforts are now directed toward the people who have
great light. He would lead them to become earthly and sensual. There are men who minister in sacred things whose
hearts are defiled with impure thoughts and unholy desires.
Married men who have children are not satisfied. They
place themselves where they invite temptation. They take
liberties that should only be taken with their lawful wives.
Thus they fall under the rebuke of God, and in the books of
heaven ''adultery'' is written opposite their names.

There should be no approach to danger. If the thoughts
were where they should be, if they were stayed upon God,
and the meditations of the soul were upon the truth and the
precious promises of God and the heavenly reward that
awaits the faithful, they would be guarded against Satan's
temptations. But, by many, vile thoughts are entertained almost constantly. They are carried into the house of God and
even into the sacred desk.

Discipline of Erring Ministers. I tell you the truth, Elder Butler, that unless there is a cleansing of the soul temple on the part of many who claim to believe and to preach the truth, God's judgments, long deferred, will come. These debasing sins have not been handled with firmness and decision. There is corruption in the soul, and, unless it is cleansed by the blood of Christ, there will be apostasies among us that will startle you.

I ask myself the question, "How is it possible for men who are opening the Scriptures to others—men who have abundance of light—men who have good ability—men who are living in the face of the judgment, upon the very borders of the eternal world—to give their thoughts and bodies to unholy practices? Well may the words of the apostle be repeated with emphasis: "Cleanse your hands, ye sinners: and purify your hearts, ye doubleminded. Be afflicted, and mourn, and weep: let your laughter be turned to mourning, and your joy to heaviness. Humble yourselves in the sight of the Lord, and He shall lift you up" (James 4:8-10).— Letter 51, 1886.

28. An Influential Minister

A Minister on a Downward Course. Elder T, my brother and fellow laborer: For two nights I have not been able to sleep many hours. About 2:00 a.m. I have been awakened greatly burdened, and after devoting some time to prayer, have attempted to write.

Your case with many others has been before me. Several years ago I was shown that your danger was very great on account of your attentions to other women besides your wife. You have indulged your own inclinations in this direction, and you stand guilty before God. The root of the whole matter is unchaste thoughts [that] are entertained which lead to improper attentions and advances, then to improper actions. All this is bad enough in men who have only a common work to do, but it is a hundredfold worse in those who have accepted sacred positions of trust.

I have in your presence dwelt particularly upon the importance of abstaining from the very appearance of evil. I have presented in your hearing the special temptations of the enemy, thinking to arouse your consciousness, that you would barricade your soul against the temptations of the enemy. I have written especially upon the dangers of young men and also of married men showing special attention to young ladies and to other men's wives. When crossing the ocean on my way to Europe, I was mightily stirred and wrote out special warnings. This was in your behalf as well as for others. It was to stop your downward course, that you should in the strength of Israel's God arise and be a man, not a plaything for the devil.

Dwarfing of Spiritual Growth by Sensual Thoughts. I was shown that in consequence of temptations you could not lift up holy hands without wrath and doubting. Your thoughts and actions crippled your endeavors; your earthliness and sensual thoughts dwarfed your spiritual growth. You are far from being the man God would have you to be, and you fail to qualify yourself for the work you might do, because your thoughts are not pure, but tainted and corrupt. Some things were shown me that are open to the eye that never slumbers nor sleeps.

This is written in the books of heaven, and in a little time your case will be decided, whether your name shall be blotted out from the Book of Life or not. It certainly will be unless you are a converted man, and humble your soul before God, and confess your sins, and turn unto the Lord with your whole heart, and purge from you every impure thought and corrupt action. Says the True Witness, "I know thy works." Do not attempt to teach the people until you are a changed man, until you have in humble penitence sought the Lord with true contrition of soul, and have a new heart.

Satan's Strong Attempts to Corrupt Ministers. I was shown that Satan would make his temptations strong to corrupt the ministers who are teaching the binding claims of the law of God. If he can tarnish the virtue, confuse the sense of purity and holiness, if he can insinuate himself into their thoughts, suggest and plan for them to sin in thought and deed against God, then their defense is gone. They have separated themselves from God; they have not the power and Spirit of God with them, and the sacred message of truth they bear to the people is not blessed of God; the seed is not watered, and the increase is not realized.

Lust as a Hindrance to the Teaching of Truth. What you need, my brother, is a pure and holy heart. Cease at once from attempting to teach the truth until you know that in the strength of God you can overcome lust. If your mind had been, in the years you have professed to be a child of God, educated and taxed to dwell upon Jesus, to pray when traveling on the cars, when walking in the streets, and wherever you were, and had you been binding about your thoughts and teaching them to dwell upon pure and holy things, I should not have to address you as I do today. The Lord must be in all your thoughts, but this work is strangely neglected.

A Minister's Work Not Like Common Business. There are some of our ministers who are engaged in active service who have some sense of the importance of the work, but there is a large number who are handling sacred truth about as they would engage in any common business. They have not been refined, ennobled, sanctified by the truth. They have not advanced step by step, growing in grace and the knowledge of Jesus Christ. They have not real, genuine faith in taking God at His word. They have not gone on from strength to a greater strength.

They have not increased in ability, but kept up the same low tone of efficiency. They have not become able men in the Scriptures, mighty men in God, and yet every privilege has been within their reach. The cause of God has not been glorified by their tame, Spiritless, Christless work. These have done great injury to the truth, and why? Because the heart is not cleansed. They have not a new, clean heart, but a heart that is open to the temptations of Satan. Such can never lead the people to the true, pure fountain of living waters. They may make others acquainted with the reasons of our faith, but it will be impossible for them to do the work which a true shepherd of the flock will do, to "feed the flock of God.". . .

Ministry of the Word Better Than Arguments. We must awaken to our God-given responsibilities. Your adversary the devil is intensely active, represented as a roaring lion, and we must be wide-awake and not ignorant of his devices. We shall surely be overcome by Satan's devices unless our hearts, our minds, our wills, are in complete subjection to the will of Christ. We shall surely fail our salvation unless the natural elements in our character, the discordant elements, are brought daily and hourly into unity with Christ's character. Unruly, debasing tendencies and passions cannot reign in the heart controlled by the Spirit of Christ. There are many who have never submitted their will and way fully, without any reserve, to Jesus Christ.

There need to be far more lessons in the ministry of the word of true conversion than of the arguments of the doctrines; for it is far easier and more natural for the heart that is not under the control of the Spirit of Christ to choose doctrinal subjects rather than the practical. There are many Christless discourses given [that are] no more acceptable to God than was the offering of Cain. They are not in harmony with God.

Taint of Spiritual Malaria. The Lord calls upon you, my brother, to step down from the work, leave the walls of Zion, or be a converted man. When your own heart is sanctified through the truth, there will be in it no moral defilement. It will now require a most desperate resistance to unholy suggestions upon your part, because your soul is tainted with spiritual malaria. You have breathed a satanic atmosphere. You have not been a man in the sight of God. When your mind should have been growing, your ideas elevated, and your plans and labors broadened, you have been growing less and less efficient as a worker, because God is not blessing your efforts.

A Crime in God's Sight. The perversion of our gifts, or their degradation to unworthy ends, is a crime in the sight of God; and yet this is constantly prevailing. The man who has capabilities for usefulness, and employs all that is winning and attractive to destroy others, to lead them astray, to bring them to a brackish, poison fountain to quench their thirst, rather than bringing them to Christ, is doing the devil's work. There are many who profess to believe the truth who are corrupt in morals and who tarnish the purity in thoughts and impulses of others, who ruin souls under the pretense of saving souls, who utter words to the unwary, Satan speaking through them, as he spoke through the serpent when he tempted Eve.

For all such there is a terrible retribution. They will reap that which they have sown. It is a terrible thing to use God's entrusted gifts, lent to bless the world, and perverted in their use, leaving a blight, a woe, a curse, instead of a blessing. But I have written largely upon this, as you have seen, in different forms.

Total Life Control Possible. And again I say, "Seek ye the Lord while He may be found, call ye upon Him while He is near: Let the wicked forsake his way, and the unrighteous man his thoughts, and let him return unto the Lord, and He will have mercy upon him; and to our God, for He will abundantly pardon" (Isa. 55:6, 7). Go to work and confess your sins before God; seek God, for you know but very little of this kind of work. Put your thoughts to work upon pure, holy subjects; tax your powers; send your supplications to heaven in earnest contrition of soul; let your conversation, your thoughts, your deportment, be in harmony with the holy faith you claim to be defending.

And when all like yourself shall repent and find the pardoning love of God, we shall see that God will work in a wonderful manner with His people. Sinners will be converted; backsliders will be reclaimed.

The Necessity for a Cleansing of Moral Defilement. I leave these lines with you. I had hoped that the great light shining from the Word of God would have been accepted, brought into your religious life, and [that] you [would] become a true, sincere Christian, doing the will of God from the heart. But I have been urged by the Spirit of the Lord to write you. The work must go forward. Everything impure must become pure and holy, or be purged from our hands; for all that is earthly, sensual, devilish, is a stumbling block to others and a curse to the cause of God.

The sooner the ranks are purged from this class, the more surely shall we see the salvation of God and the power of the truth in our midst. It is because we are loaded down with those who have not been partakers of the divine nature, who have failed to escape the corruption that is in the world through lust, that we have so much weakness and feebleness in our midst. We must arouse. We must cleanse the camp of Israel of its moral defilement.—Letter 5, 1886.

Public Exposure Not Always Necessary. I do not want, unless necessary, that the case of T shall be made public. I have a response from him which acknowledges the testimony, but I do not want, for the sake of his wife and children, to make [it] public. I pity the man sincerely, and if I could do anything to recover either of these men from the snare of the devil, I would do so. T takes a far better position than Canright. Although both of these men have made many falsehoods against me and our people, I am not embittered against them and do not wish to injure [them], for I bear in mind that there is a judgment when every man's work will be brought in review before God, and every man will receive of the great Judge according to his works.— Letter 59, 1889.

29. Four Unholy Ministers

*Satan's Devices.** I have much to say to you. You have been represented to me as being in great peril. Satan is on your track, and at times he has whispered to you pleasing fables, and has shown you charming pictures of one whom he represents as a more suitable companion for you than the wife of your youth, the mother of your children.

Satan is working stealthily, untiringly, to effect your

---

*Written to a minister who was fantasizing regarding a woman not his wife, with whom he was sentimentally involved. He thought of living with this woman and having children by her in heaven.

downfall through his specious temptations. He is determined to become your teacher, and you need now to place yourself where you can get strength to resist him. He hopes to lead you into the maze of spiritualism. He hopes to wean your affections from your wife, and to fix them upon another woman. He desires that you shall allow your mind to dwell upon this woman until through unholy affection she becomes your god.

Fantasy About Families in Heaven. The enemy of souls has gained much when he can lead the imagination of one of Jehovah's chosen watchmen to dwell upon the possibilities of association in the world to come, with some woman whom he loves, and of there raising up a family. We need no such pleasing pictures. All such views originate in the mind of the tempter.

We have the plain assurance of Christ that in the world to come, the redeemed "neither marry, nor are given in marriage, neither can they die any more; for they are equal unto the angels; and are the children of God, being the children of the resurrection" (Luke 20:35, 36).

It is presented to me that spiritual fables are taking many captive. Their minds are sensual, and, unless a change comes, this will prove their ruin. To all who are indulging in these unholy fancies I would say, Stop, for Christ's sake, stop right where you are. You are on forbidden ground. Repent, I entreat of you, and be converted.

First Place in a Husband's Affections. To married men I am instructed to say, "It is to your wives, the mothers of your children, that your respect and affection are due. Your attentions are to be given to them, and your thoughts are to dwell upon plans for their happiness. . . ."

My brother U, remember that the woman who receives the least manifestation of affection from a man who is the husband of another woman, shows herself to be in need of repentance and conversion. And the man who allows his wife to occupy the second place in his affections is dishonoring himself and his God. This thing is one of the signs of the last days. But surely you do not desire to fulfill this sign. This is the part that the wicked are to act. Christ will take charge of the affections of those who love and honor God, causing them to center upon proper objects.

My brother, your wife has her faults, but so have you. She is your wife still. She is the mother of your children, and you are to respect, cherish, and love her. Guard yourself carefully, that impurity may not abide in mind or heart. . . .

True as Steel to the Marriage Vow. Brother U, your case was presented to me some time ago, but I have delayed writing, thinking that I might see you and talk with you. You are being imprisoned with a dangerous sentimentalism, and this has nearly spoiled you and the one also who has permitted you to make her your favorite. You need not ask God to bless you in pursuing this course. In this matter your mind has been worked by the enemy who stands ready to control those who give place to spiritualistic affection.

You have a wife, and you are bound to her by the law of God. "Ye have heard that it was said by them of old time, Thou shalt not commit adultery: but I say unto you, That whosoever looketh on a woman to lust after her hath committed adultery with her already in his heart. . . . It hath been said, Whosoever shall put away his wife, let him give her a writing of divorcement: but I say unto you, That whosoever shall put away his wife, saving for the cause of fornication, causeth her to commit adultery: and whosoever shall marry her that is divorced committeth adultery" (Matt. 5:27-32).

May the Lord help you is my prayer. Now is the time to

fight the good fight of faith. Now is the time to wrestle against the prompting of the natural heart. Now is your time to be as true as steel to your marriage vows, refusing, in thought, word, or deed, to spoil your record as a man who fears God and obeys His commandments. You have been imbibing spiritualistic ideas. But if you will now turn wholly to God, the grace of our Lord Jesus Christ will be imparted to you, and truth will triumph in your life.—Letter 231, 1903.

*A Public Reproof.** We have some hard labor to do here. There was a spirit of lightness [on the ground]. The young men were mating [pairing] up [with] the young girls, and when reproved, were, some of them, defiant, hardhearted, reckless. We had to get this cleared away before we could get the spirit of freedom into our meeting. But Sabbath everything seemed to break away. Elder Y, who has been preaching, has been running after the girls, married women, and widows, and this seemed to be his inclination out of the desk from State to State. Sunday morning I called him out by name and told him and all present we had no use for any such men, for they would only make the work of the burden-bearing laborers double what it is now.

If they would only take themselves out of the way and act out just what was in their heart, without doing this evil work under a pretense of godliness, the cause would be relieved. He has made no confession yet. Do not know as he will do so. But light came into our meetings, and the young who had been following his example came out decidedly and confessed their wrong course of action. When will those who profess Christ be wise?—Letter 53, 1884.

_____

*Written to a young unmarried minister.

*Invitation to Work in Another Country.** Dear Brother V: I have this morning received and read your letter, and if I do not answer at once I fear it will pass from my mind. . . .

In regard to your changing your location, I would mention to you England. There is a large field and but few workers, plenty of work to be done in which all may act a part—all of your family, if they desire to give themselves to the Lord and act a part in His cause. You will find room enough to work, and if you go forth to labor in meekness and humility, redeeming the past errors of your life, God will accept you. There is need of laborers in England, and the advantage of that country over other parts of Europe is that our American brethren do not have to work through an interpreter. . . .

Should you come to England you will certainly find work enough to do, and God is merciful; He pities our weakness; He forgives our transgressions; and, if we will only live humble and penitent, if we will cease from evil and do well, the Lord will approve. May the Lord teach you and work for you.

I wish that there were many more men who would give themselves to the missionary work in England. That kingdom has but few workers. We want missionaries whom God can work with and bless. We want men who will feel the burden of souls, men who will work as Christ worked, zealously, disinterestedly, to save sinners and enlighten those in darkness. I write this short letter to you, thinking it is as well as more that might be written. Your sister in Christ.—Letter 41, 1886.

---

*A letter written to a repentant minister who had broken the seventh commandment.

*Impure Thoughts and Imaginings.** Elder Z, I have much distress of soul for you. I fear, yes, greatly fear, you will never enter into the kingdom of God. I have much pain at heart as I consider your case, standing in the light of the delegated servant of Jesus Christ, yet so clouded with defilement that holy angels cannot come near you. It is no new thing that your thoughts are corrupted by impure desires and imaginings. You have not dismissed unlawful desires and lustful thoughts. When you met me in Healdsburg and told me that you had gained the victory, you told me a falsehood, for you knew this was not the truth.

The Fly in the Spider's Web. Your past life had been presented before me as one who had no internal strength to resist evil if it put on an inviting aspect. You have obtained the confidence of women in you as a man of piety and righteousness, then you have taken advantage of this confidence to take liberties with them—kissing them, and going just as far with them in seductive, lustful practices as they would allow you to go, not only with Sister X but with others. And I am pained to the heart when I consider that you have tainted and polluted more than one or two or three or four with your insinuations and your fawning and caressing which have led souls to dissipation and vice. And you a watchman, you a shepherd! . . .

You have made evil and lustful practices appear harmless, and some have been led away with their own lust and enticed because they had not moral courage to rebuke you, a minister, for your iniquitous practices. There have been not a few who have sacrificed conscience, peace of mind, and the favor of God, because a man whom the people have

---

*Written to an unrepentant minister.

set as a watchman on the walls of Zion has been their tempter—a wolf in sheep's clothing.

And these who had been uncorrupted fall into the snare [which] Satan, through the bad shepherd, has set for them under different pretenses and excuses. You have hid your evil heart of deadly opposition to purity and holiness. The fly enticed into the spider's web, the fish which is lured on by the bait on the hook, has been ensnared and taken.

Erroneous Approach to Marriage Counseling. You have by your course of action debased sacred things to the level of the common. Many have come near being ruined who have, as it were, been plucked as a brand from the burning; but the performance of yours to break down the barriers which preserve the sanctity of the family relation between husband and wife, the arranged plans to make the wife communicate to you the secrets of her married life, induce those who are yielding in disposition, who have become captivated with you, to open their heart to you as to a Catholic confessor; and you encourage in them the thought that they have made a mistake in the married life.

In every family there are at times misunderstandings. There are thoughts and feelings expressed that Satan takes advantage of, but if both husband and wife will resist the devil and humble their hearts before God, then the difficulties soon will be healed without leaving ugly scars. But you have done a work to encourage alienation in the place of healing the difficulties; and peace of mind, harmony, and the usefulness not only of women but of men has been destroyed, and the seeds of licentious practices that you have sown have produced a bitter, bitter harvest. The wanderings from God in this way are common, but the fact is, so few return.

Sacred Interwoven With the Impure. The coy, complying

disposition of women or girls to the advances and familiarity of men, married men, leads them to be easily entrapped. The man who should watch for souls in order to save them, watches for opportunities and occasions to ruin them. There are so many who have little fixedness of principle, who come into contact with the men who preach the truth; and some of these educate and refine iniquity before them, clothing it in angel robes, and as their own hearts are not garrisoned with fixed, unswerving principles, the work of ruin is speedily accomplished.

The sacred is brought down and so interwoven with lust and impure, unholy practices that the victim is confused, and the soul temple becomes a sink of iniquity. At first the unsuspecting only listen; they receive the liberties of preference shown them; then the education goes on until "as an ox goeth to the slaughter, or as a fool to the correction of the stocks" (Prov. 7:22), they follow in the steps of the tempter and go fully as far as he would lead them.— Letter 82, 1886.

30. Ellen White's Assistants

*To W. F. C., September 6, 1895.** This morning as I came from the school ground I saw your horse fastened to a tree before the tent occupied by Fannie Y. After a while I went to the tent. A lady from Newcastle and Jessie Israel were visiting Fannie. You were sitting down, writing on the typewriter. Why did you not take the typewriter at once into the dining tent? What impression can such a course make

---

*Both Brother W. F. C. and Fannie Y were employees of Ellen White, first at Melbourne, and later at Cooranbong, New South Wales. In 1895 Mrs. White and her staff were living and working in tents while Sunnyside, the permanent residence, was being built.

upon the mind of the young girl visiting at the school? It made an impression that was anything but favorable.

Your freedom with young women is improper, but it is so natural and common to you that you think nothing of it. The word of God has told you that you are to abstain from the very appearance of evil; but do you? You are a married man, with a wife and two boys, whom you have left in America, and this fact should be sufficient, without any further prompting, to lead you to cultivate sobriety and carefulness in your association with others. . . . I write these things to you because you are deceiving Fannie, and she is apparently totally blind and infatuated. . . .

Placing yourself in the society of Fannie as much as you did while at Melbourne had not only the appearance of evil, but was evil. You enjoyed it, but you should have had discernment to understand that by your course of action you were encouraging others in the same path.

I am now going to Tasmania, and you and Fannie will remain at Avondale. After my absence, you will feel inclined to associate together more freely, because I am not present to hold the fort. I fear you will dishonor the truth by your familiarity. I decidedly protest against this. Keep yourself out of Fannie's tent, or else a scandal will be created.— Letter 17, 1895.

To W. F. C., c. September 1895. I have had very little help from Fannie for many months, not because she cannot work, but her association with you has caused her to have an experience which has unfitted her to do anything in my work. . . .

I feel deeply over another matter, and that is your visiting Fannie in her tent. I have already decided that you two cannot work together. You are a married man, father of two children. If your wife has obtained a divorce from you, that does not leave you free to marry again, as I read my Bible. . . .

Before leaving I must lay down some rules. There is no call for W. F. C. to visit Fannie's tent. Fannie has not been in working order for some time. Her association with you is largely the cause of this. I know this to be so, and therefore I say, Keep away from her tent. When I am away you will feel that you have a fine opportunity to get into her society whenever you can; and I cannot go without warning you and charging you to keep yourself to yourself. I want no reproach brought upon me nor upon this community by imprudent, careless habits or practices.—Letter 19, 1896.

To Fannie Y, November 23, 1895. I have been considering your case in connection with W. F. C., and I have no other counsel to give than I have given. I consider that you have no moral right to marry W. F. C.; he has no moral right to marry you. He left his wife after giving her great provocation. He left her whom he had vowed before God to love and cherish while both should live. Before ever she obtained her divorce, when she was his lawful wife, he left her for three years, and then left her in heart, and expressed his love to you. The matter has been negotiated largely between you and a married man, while he was legally bound to the wife he married, who has had two children by him.

I see not a particle of leniency in the Scriptures given either of you to contract marriage, although his wife is divorced. From the provocation he has given her, it was largely his own course of action that has brought this result, and I cannot see in any more favorable light his having a legal right to link his interest with yours or you to link your interest with his. One thing is settled. I could not connect with either of you if this step is taken, for I see this matter in a light that the Scriptures would condemn your connection. Therefore, I wish you both to understand that from the light God has given me regarding the past and the present, I could not think of employing either of you if you take this step.

I am astonished that you should for a moment give thought to such a thing, and place your affections on a married man who had left his wife and children under such circumstances. I advise you to lay your thoughts and plans regarding this matter just as they are before our responsible brethren, that you may receive their counsel, and let them show you from the law of God the error into which you have fallen. You have both broken the law even in thinking that you might unite in marriage. You should have repelled the thought at its first suggestion.—Letter 14, 1895.

To James Edson White, December 9, 1895. . . . But oh, the heartache, for other things were developing and being made manifest which had been a fearful strain on me. It was the intimacy between W. F. C. and [Fannie]. I had presented before them all the dangers, but they denied it. But at the meeting at Melbourne Fannie acknowledged she loved W. F. C. and he loved her. I tried to present the matter before them in its true bearing. W. F. C. had a wife living. Recently she obtained a divorce. He had left her and been gone three years. But Fannie told me she had been praying that if it was right she should marry W. F. C. that his wife might obtain a divorce. What blindness will come to those who begin to depart from a straightforward course! These two had thought they could unite in marriage and they could both unite in carrying on my work. The management of all my business would be supposed to be in his hands. Not much, I told them. Such a step would cut them off from me forever, both of them, because W. F. C. had no moral right to [marry].—Letter 123a, 1895.

To W. F. C., April 9, 1896. I am greatly distressed as I review the past, and as matters are brought to my notice by the Spirit of God. I have a decided message to bear to you, Brother C. Special light in regard to you and your family was not given me until about two years ago. I was then shown that the attitude you manifested in your home life was unchristian. You began your married life by accepting a false sabbath, and by sailing under false colors. But a wife that was obtained by selling principles of truth could not bring peace or happiness to the purchaser. God was dishonored by your action in this matter, and His truth was trampled in the dust.

When you gave up the Sabbath for your wife, she rejoiced that she had gained a victory, and Satan also rejoiced. But when she accepted a man who was willing to sell his Lord for her, she could not look up to him and honor him as a wife should honor her husband. When she married you under these circumstances, she did not distinguish between a heaven-born love and an earthly love, not of divine origin. A man who will sacrifice his love for his heavenly Father for a wife will also sell his wife for another woman. This quality of love is base; it is of this earth, and will never bear the test of trial.

The Lord does not revise the laws of His government, the laws which control His subjects both in this world and in the heavenly universe. Natural laws must be obeyed. But you were so determined to obtain your wife that you broke down every barrier, and broke God's law by yielding up the Sabbath; and you have been reaping only that which you have sown.

After marrying your wife, you again accepted the Sabbath. This was the right move to make if you made it in sincerity and in the fear of God. Said Christ [John 14:21, 23, quoted].

But you secured your wife under a promise which you afterwards broke. You paid a dear price for her, and by breaking your word you have given her every reason to be tempted. Thus Satan has had every opportunity to deceive her, and he has presented this matter to her in his own light. You sacrificed the truth and sold your allegiance to God to obtain a wife, and after you again commenced keeping the Sabbath, your course toward your wife should have been entirely different from what it has been. You should have shown her all the tenderness, forbearance, and love which you manifested toward her before your marriage. But this was not done. You did not pursue a course which would keep her love. I myself cannot put confidence in you as a Christian, and under present developments, I could not give my consent for you to become a member of any church.

You thought that when you were once married you could do as you pleased. This has embittered your married life, and your wife has had every reason for refusing to leave her home and come to you to this country. Your acceptance of fanatical views was nothing in your favor, and gave your wife an opportunity to strengthen herself against the principles of truth.

For years you have been away from your home. Leaving as you did was a wrong against your family. You have told me that you would never humiliate yourself by going back, *never*. But the Lord has presented this matter before me. I know that you cannot be clear in the sight of God until you do all in your power to be reconciled to your wife. You have a work to do in your family which cannot be left undone. This I stated to you last September. Whatever position your wife has taken, whatever course of recklessness and levity she has pursued, this does not excuse you from acting a father's part to your children. You ought to go back to your home and do all in your power to heal the breach, which you, a professed believer in the truth, have done more than your wife to make.

When you placed your love upon another woman, even though your wife had obtained a divorce, you transgressed the seventh commandment. But you have done worse than this. You loved another woman before your wife obtained a divorce, and you have said to one, "How hard it is to be bound to a woman I do not love, when there is one I love, yes, the very ground she walks on."

Your course while in my family was not open and frank. The transactions between you and the one upon whom you placed your affections were carried on under falsehood and deception. In the guise of false pretension, secret plans were carried out. The Lord opened these matters before me, and I tried to change the order of things, but the burden of soul was to you and others accounted a thing of naught. At this time you were giving Bible readings, and taking a prominent part in church work. My advice and counsel was not asked in regard to this important decision. Had I been, I should have been spared much pain that followed.

When I talked with you in regard to your freedom in the company of young ladies, and told you that I could not have you in my family while I went to Tasmania, your answer was that you had always been sociable with young women, and had never thought that there was any harm in it. I told you that I knew there was harm in this freedom and that I could not feel justified in leaving you in my family while I was absent.

When I told you that you could not remain in my family, you said that after settling your accounts, which would take about a week, you could go. But this matter dragged along, or was neglected, till about two weeks before our return from Tasmania, and then in July we went to Cooranbong.

This matter cannot rest here. I cannot be looked upon as keeping you from your home and family. It was a mistake, I think, to bring you into my family at all. I did this to help you, but I cannot let it be represented to others that we consider you a man worthy to engage in the sacred work which the Lord has given me. I cannot have this matter appear thus, for it places me in a wrong light.

I cannot appear to justify your course of action in your married life. Leaving your wife and family is an offense to God, and I must present this matter as it is, before the president of your conference, Elder Williams. I had hoped that when you saw your delusion you would feel that repentance for your course of action that needeth not to be repented of. But my experience at Armadale, and the burden brought upon me there, made me a great sufferer; and matters in regard to your past life have been more fully opened before me. . . . You have thought that you would receive the credentials of a minister of the gospel, but had these been given you, reproach would have been brought upon the cause of God. You have represented yourself as being a wronged man, but it is your wife who has been most wronged. She should never have been treated as you have treated her. You pursued such a course toward your little ones that your wife could not but be estranged from you. Her heart was wounded, bruised, and she was almost distracted by your overbearing, masterly government in discipline of your children.

After giving up Fannie you placed your affections upon

another. This shows just what you would do if opportunities presented themselves. You show young girls attention and thus win their love, for if you choose, your manner can be very gracious and attractive. As these things have passed before me, I have felt indignant. I cannot, will not, keep silent on these matters. I determined that you should be un-veiled as an unprincipled man. Your ideas of what a Christian should be are so much unlike the principles laid down in the Word of God that no responsibility in connection with the cause of God should be given you.—Letter 18, 1896.

To Elder I. N. Williams, President of the Pennsylvania Conference [W. F. C.'s home conference], April 12, 1896. We have had great trouble of mind in regard to Brother W. F. C., who expects to return to America by this month's boat. He has shown a fondness for the society of young girls, and has been full of gaiety, conducting himself like a boy. About a year ago, at the suggestion of my son, W. C. White, I employed him to run the typewriter for Fannie Y, as she read the manuscript to him. But soon I became bur-dened. Warnings were given to me again and again. I talked with him by himself in regard to his freedom and enjoyment in the society of young women and his frivolous conduct, but he said he had always been sociable with young ladies and thought it no harm.

We wanted to help him, for he had no money and but very poor clothing. He has good ability, and might have developed into a competent helper for W. C. [White] or a worker for me. But I dared not have him remain a member of my family.

He became attached to Fannie Y and the matter was car-ried on under a deception before he learned that his wife had obtained a divorce. When he heard this he seemed greatly relieved, for his heart was fully weaned from her. But the Lord gave me light in regard to the matter. I consider that he is far more to blame than his wife in view of the fact that he claims to believe sacred truth, and she makes no such profession. He has not been a kind, tender husband; he has not been patient and forbearing, but very critical and overbearing if his wife displeased him in any way. I cannot see how his wife, in contact with his temperament and disposition, could feel drawn toward the truth. She has opposed him and has made it hard for him, but not a whit harder than he has made it for her by his course of action. He has not taken opposition patiently, or as a Christian should. He did wrong when he left his home and his wife and children. A few months ago I learned that he had done nothing for their support.

As matters were unfolded to me, it was a most serious matter for him to allow his affections to center upon another woman when he had a wife living, whom he had promised to love and cherish as long as they both should live. Why he should leave his home so long has been a mystery to us all, until recently I have had divine enlightenment.

He can appear very attractive, and win the confidence and favor of the girls, but when crossed he has such a temper and disposition that, unless he is changed, no woman, believer or unbeliever, could live peaceably with him. He would pursue a course that would make any woman miserable. He is an intemperate eater, and this is why he has so little patience.

I felt that the time had come when I should no longer employ him to transact my business, for warnings kept coming to me from the Lord concerning his course of action.

I will write further in regard to this if necessary. Please write to me, stating facts concerning the family there, as far as you know. Help W. F. C., if you can, to set things right and remove this reproach from the cause of God. Even if his wife is already married, it may be there is something he can do for his children.—Letter 104, 1896.

To Brother and Sister G. C. Tenney, July 1, 1897. The work between Fannie Y and Brother W. F. C. was begun at the Melbourne camp meeting [January, 1894]. There she became enamored of a married man, with two children. She utterly denied that there was any affection between her and Brother C. She stood before me in my tent and declared that there was nothing to the reports. For one year after this she was good for nothing to me, only a dead, heavy load. . . .

We had the affair between Fannie and W. F. C. all through the Armadale camp meeting. I talked with them both separately, and told them that the Lord had a controversy with them both. They denied that there was anything like particular attachment between them. I knew better; but the Lord helped me to work through the meeting. Just before the meeting closed, Fannie came to me and said, "Oh, Sister White, I have come to you as to a mother. I do love Brother C with all my heart, and my heart is just broken. Three times has this cup of bliss been presented to me, and then been snatched away." Then the girl said, "I prayed that if it was right for us to get married, his wife might get a divorce from him, and it was not many weeks before she did get a divorce. Now don't you think the Lord heard my prayer?" I dared not talk with her, for I had to speak that day before a large congregation. If Sister Prescott is in Battle Creek, she will be able to tell you the particulars.

Well, from that time I cut loose from Fannie, never, as I thought, to connect with her again. But a little while after this, Fannie was in Sydney and wrote me another confession. I thought that I could not take her back, but the Spirit of the Lord rested upon me, and said, "Give her another trial." So I decided that I would see Fannie and tell her that I would take her back. This I did, and she remained with me several weeks, but was not able to do any work; then she decided that she wanted to go home to her mother, and I told her that she might feel free to do so.—Letter 114, 1897.

SECTION VIII

UNSCRIPTURAL MARRIAGES

31. Respect for Unbiblical Marriages

Separation Not Recommended. Dear Brother [C. H. Bliss]: Your letter has been received and read. I have had acquaintance with several such cases and have found those who felt conscientious to do something in similar cases to the one you mention. After having stirred things up generally, and torn things to pieces, they had no wisdom to put things together to make matters better. I found that those who were so zealous to tear things down did nothing to build them up in right order. They had the faculty to confuse, distress, and create a most deplorable condition of things, but not the faculty to make them better.

You have asked my counsel in regard to this case. I would say that unless those who are burdened in reference to the matter have carefully studied a better arrangement, and can find places for these where they can be comfortable, they better not carry out their ideas of a separation. I hope to learn that this matter is not pressed, and that sympathy will not be withdrawn from the two whose interests have been united.

No Hasty Movements. I write this because I have seen so many cases of the kind, and persons would have great burden till everything was unsettled and uprooted, and then their interest and burden went no further. We should individually know that we have a zeal that is according to knowledge. We should not move hastily in such matters, but look on every side of the question. We should move very cautiously and with pitying tenderness, because we do not know all the circumstances which led to this course of action.

I advise that these unfortunate ones be left to God and their own consciences, and that the church shall not treat them as sinners until they have evidence that they are such in the sight of the holy God. He reads hearts as an open book. He will not judge as man judgeth.—Letter 5, 1891.*

32. Brother G

[*W. C. White Statement*: "Regarding Brother G, I can speak quite freely. About 1875 he married a very brilliant schoolteacher. . . . She was very talented, but after a number of years she became quarrelsome and made his life miserable. At that time he was associated with a very brilliant young woman who was an accountant at X College, and formed a fondness

---

*Just twenty years later W. C. White wrote another correspondent:

"Mother has received during the last twenty years many letters making inquiry regarding the matters about which you write, and she has many times written in reply that she had no advice to give different from that of the apostle Paul. Recently she has refused to deal with letters of this character, and tells us not to bring them to her attention.

"My own views regarding this matter, which I believe to be in harmony with the counsel that I have heard Mother give to individuals years ago, and which I believe to be in harmony with views of the leading brethren and with the teaching of the Scripture, is that there is no blessing to come by our breaking up families who may have sinned or been sinned against before or since they embraced present truth."—W. C. White letter to Elder G. W. Anglebarger, October 6, 1911.

for her. Sister White wrote him a very plain warning, which he promised to heed. Shortly after Sister White had gone to Europe, Brother G resigned his position at X College, went to Michigan to visit his sister, and offered no obstruction to his wife in getting a divorce.

"Thus far, those who knew the case approved, but shortly after this he married the bookkeeper before mentioned; then all his friends were greatly grieved. He taught a while at _____, then settled near _____, and for many years worked very hard, his wife helping him to make a living on a little fruit and vegetable farm. They came to see the wickedness of the course they had taken. They repented of it very bitterly, and their brethren and sisters were satisfied that their repentance was genuine. They had three beautiful children growing up, and no one, as far as I know, encouraged them to separate. When the matter was put before Sister White, she did not encourage a separation, nor could she encourage any movement to exclude him from participation in the work of the third angel's message. In his later life he labored in a humble way in self-supporting work in the South.

"If persons living in the light of the third angel's message purpose to leave one companion for the sake of uniting with someone else, it is our duty to warn and reprove and discipline.

"If persons before embracing the message have entangled themselves, and afterward have repented, confessed their sins, received forgiveness of God, and won the confidence of their brethren, it is better for both ministers and laymen to leave them alone, enjoying the forgiveness and justification which have been wrought through Christ, without undertaking to tear up existing relations."— February 21, 1927.

Elder White later added, "It has been my belief for a long time that our brethren make a serious mistake in their efforts to break up families by arguing that in the fulfillment of their vows, made unwisely in most cases, that they are continually, day by day, committing adultery."—W. C. White letter, January 6, 1931.

Ellen White's attitude toward Brother G is revealed in the letters that follow.]

Oh, for Wisdom From on High! Dear Brother Haskell: . . . We consider the opening [of the Bible School at Melbourne] was good. All are pleased with the buildings and location for the school. This is rather remarkable, for generally some have criticisms to make, but we have not heard one word of dissatisfaction expressed or even intimated.

We had conversation after the meeting with Elder Starr. The question was in reference to a teacher of grammar for the advanced classes. There is no perplexity in regard to the first classes of grammar, but we need well-qualified teachers in all branches, and we hope Elder Olsen will find either a man or woman that can come to Australia as a thorough teacher. If only G had kept himself straight, he would be just the one to come. But the question is whether his record will not follow him. We scarcely dare venture the matter and run the risk. That the man has sincerely repented I have not a doubt, and I believe the Lord has forgiven him. But if obliged to make explanations it would not be an easy matter to do; so what shall we do with G? Leave him where he is, a prey to remorse, and to be useless the remainder of his life? I cannot see what can be done. Oh, for wisdom from on high! Oh, for the counsel of One who reads the heart as an open book! How Satan watches for souls to bind them with his hellish cords that they become lost to the work and almost helpless in his hands. "Watch and pray, lest ye enter into temptation."—Letter 13, 1892. (Written five years after Brother G's unscriptural marriage.)

Invitation to Another Country. Dear Brother G: I have had my mind drawn out for you time and again. Had I felt at liberty to exercise my judgment, I should have given my counsel a long time ago for you to change your location. I had hoped my brethren would have had wisdom from above to give counsel to you that you should not be where you are today. If you have anything to do, it must be soon. Were you in this country [Australia], I fully believe you would see doors opening where you could be at work to be a lightbearer to those who are in the darkness of error.

How would it be should you come to this country? Like Abraham, going out not knowing whither he went, and humbly seeking guidance, I plead that you make a break. Come here to Australia, while we are here. Come on your own responsibility. You will have means, if you sell your farm, to bring you here. Then I believe the way will open for you to work, and may the Lord direct you, is my earnest wish and sincere prayer. . . .

There is work in abundance for you to do in the great harvest field. Here are fields all ripe for the harvest, work to be entered upon in Sydney, of about a million people, and Melbourne numbering still more. There is Queensland to be entered. There are thirty Sabbathkeepers in one place in Queensland that have never seen nor heard the living preacher, and others are scattered all through that region, waiting for the message of truth.

Will you please consider this matter, and write us what you think? What are your finances? What are you thinking of doing? How is the Lord leading your mind? Please consider the matter, and may the Lord give you wisdom to move somewhere at once. In much love.—Letter 7a, 1894.

Following the Lord's Leading. Dear Brother and Sister G: I am pleased to hear from you, and to learn that you are endeavoring to be of still greater service to the cause of God. It is your privilege to receive a rich blessing in helping others. You may be "diligent in business," and also "fervent in spirit, serving the Lord." You may help your associates in the exercise of your judgment, and by inculcating the principles of economy. We must spend money judiciously, and I believe that you will endeavor to do this.

Be ever hopeful, and increase in the grace and wisdom of Christ. I am more than pleased that you can engage in school work and unite your influence with other workers in opening the Scriptures to those who do not understand the Word of God. I believe that the Lord has been leading you.—Letter 56, 1910.

33. Stephen Belden

[*W. C. White Statement*: "Sister White did not sympathize with those who took the ground that a person who had separated from a companion on other than Scriptural ground, and married again, that this second marriage must be broken up if they were to be accepted or retained in an SDA church.

"Sister White fully recognized that these people in most cases had sinned, that some had sinned grievously, and that they should not be accepted into fellowship of our churches unless that sin was repented of. Sister White did not accept the contention that such repentance could not be genuine without breaking the new bond, and making an earnest effort to return to former companions. She recognized the fact that in most instances a reunion with the parties formerly connected with in marriage would be either impossible or exceedingly unprofitable. She also recognized that the vows entered into in the second marriage called for such an action as was most merciful and kind to the contracting parties.

"She sometimes referred to the teaching of Paul, who having reached a certain point in his experience, said, 'But I spare you.' He knew there were existing conditions that people were living in relations resulting from sin. He also knew that Christ would accept their genuine repentance, and that in many cases it would make matters worse if existing relations were torn up to prepare a way for a reunion with the parties who were incompanionable, so Sister White used to say, 'But I spare you.'

"Sister White's next older sister, Sarah Harmon, was married to Stephen Belden and became the mother of five children. After her death, in pity for his children, he married a woman who had many years been a faithful servant in his household. Shortly after this, the measles visited the vicinity, and she with others had the measles in a severe form. The measles went to her brain, and she became insane, and had to be take to the asylum. Brother Belden struggled along for some time, trying to care for his five children,

then for their sake married a very good, efficient
woman. She helped him make a home and bring up
his children, and was with him in Norfolk Island
when he died. At various times, individuals where
Brother Belden lived undertook to secure his ex-
clusion from the church because he had married
without separation from his wife on the charge of
adultery. When appealed to in regard to this matter,
Sister White said, 'Let them alone.' ''—W. C. White
letter, January 6, 1931.]

34. William E (Part I)

[William E was born in Melborn, Quebec, in
1856. After attending Battle Creek College he labored
as a minister or colporteur in Michigan, Illinois, In-
diana, Tennessee, and Alabama.

His first marriage ended in divorce, after which he
fathered a child by a second woman without marrying
her. Then, on August 5, 1892, he married a third
woman, who was still his companion when he died in
1934.

In 1901 William E's father and brother insisted
that he should divorce his wife and return to an earlier
companion. His first wife had remarried but the
second woman, who was the mother of his il-
legitimate daughter, was anxious to marry him.

Edson White wrote his mother on October 30,
1901, and asked if it was necessary for Brother E to
leave his current wife in order to get right with God.
Ellen White's response follows.]

I have just read your letter concerning Will E. I regard
the matter in the same light that you do, and think it a cruel,

wicked thing that the father of Will E should take the course that he is taking, but I have not dared to answer his letters. If anything can come from me through you to him, I would say that his case cannot be improved by leaving the present wife. It would not better the case to go to the other woman in the question. . . .

I have not written to Will E, but know that if the father would repent before God and do his first works, and cease to consider himself as one that can help his son, he would ask himself the question, "Is my name written there, on the page white and fair?" He might well begin to humble himself before God, and leave Will Wales with God.

Let the father and brother make diligent work for themselves. They both need the converting power of God. May the Lord help these poor souls to remove spot and stain from their own characters, and repent of their wrongs, and leave Will E with the Lord.

I am so sorry for the man, for his course is in such a shape that it will not answer to be meddled with, for there are difficulties upon difficulties. I would say that the Lord understands the situation, and if Will E will seek Him with all his heart, He will be found of him. If he will do his best, God will pardon and receive him.

Oh, how precious it is to know that we have One who does know and understand, and will help the ones who are most helpless. But the rebuke of God is upon the father and the brother who would drive to destruction and perdition one who stands in the sight of God under no worse condemnation than themselves, and yet they will so use their gifts of speech as to dishearten, discourage, and drive Will E to despair.

Will E may hope in God and do the best he can to serve God in all humility of mind, casting his helpless soul upon the great Sin Bearer. I have not written a word to either father or son. I would gladly do something to help poor Will E to make things right, but this cannot be done as matters are now situated, without someone's being wronged.

I understand perfectly the situation between Will E and his first wife . . . and I knew how the case would terminate, for Will E cannot endure to be a slave, his identity lost in a wife who made herself his judge in conscience, in his duty, and in his work generally.—Letter 175, 1901.

Section IX

COUNSELS TO CHURCH ADMINISTRATORS

35. William E (Part II)

[On August 15, 1911, Elder C. F. McVagh, president of the Southern Union Conference, wrote W. C. White:

"Dear Brother: In Alabama the conference officers are much perplexed about the case of William E, and I have been asked to write for a copy of what has been written [by Ellen White] bearing upon his public labor as a minister, and also for present advice, or instruction from the Lord. You are acquainted with his past. His life has been straight so far as is known for several years, and he has sold books and Bibles. But he feels a burden to preach and wherever he goes he soon has opportunity to preach. He has wonderful ability and soon there is an interest. He gives outward evidence of deep consecration and people accept the truth under his labors.

"A little over a year ago he moved to Birmingham, Alabama, and soon was taking an active part in church work. The church at that time was very much run down. He became elder, and soon had some work started and several families interested. The interest grew and during the winter he held Sunday night meetings in a theater with a large attendance, and some accepted the truth. He had the confidence of the church members who were naturally much encouraged, and so, as he had to devote much of his time to taking care of the interest (he is an indefatigable worker), the conference committee voted him $8 a week to assist him. Of course he cannot live on that, and he thinks the interest demands full time, and he is really looking to the restoration of his credentials and complete recognition as a minister of the conference. His present experience no one doubts, but the past has marked him and his family.

"His wife is a nervous wreck and her confidence has been so shaken that while she wants him to preach, there is constant danger that as he becomes popular and mingles with the people that she will become jealous, whether [there] is any cause or not, and herself bring on a scandal by talking and telling of the past which she is prone to do when she becomes suspicious of him. All would be greatly relieved if there is any definite counsel from the Lord. I feel sure that all would accept it, including Brother and Sister E.

"Personally, I feel very sorry for them both and have confidence that they are trying to live right, and I wish to encourage them in every way that is right. His past is so checkered and so widely known that we fear to advise him to labor in the ministry, but the fact is he is doing it, and the Lord apparently blesses his efforts. Shall we advise him to quit preaching, or shall the conference accept his labor and pay him for it? If he labors he must be paid and then what about his credentials?

Sincerely
(Signed) C. F. McVagh

"Written at the request of the Alabama Conference Committee."

On September 14, Elder White placed this letter in Mrs. White's hands, and on September 15, Elder White conveyed Mrs. White's counsel in the case to Elder McVagh. W. C. White's letter is as follows:

"Dear Brother McVagh: It is two or three weeks since I received your letter of August 15, regarding the perplexity which has arisen in the Alabama Conference over the case of William E.

"Since our return from southern California, Mother has been weak and weary, and I did not place this letter in her hands until yesterday. Then she read it all through, and when she recalled the sad experiences through which Brother E has passed, she felt very sorry for him and for our brethren whose hearts have been made sad through the past years by his weak and wicked course.

"Mother says that those who have dealt with the perplexities arising from his many transgressions in the past should take the responsibility of advising regarding our present duty toward him. Mother does not wish to take large responsibility in this matter, but she says regarding Elder E as she has said regarding other men in a somewhat similar position, if they have thoroughly repented, if they are living such lives as convince their brethren that they are thoroughly in earnest, do not cut them off from fellowship, do not forbid their working for Christ in a humble capacity, but do not elevate them to positions of responsibility.

"From this I would understand that it would be

unwise to renew his credentials and send him from place to place among the people, but if he has by a faithful Christian life won the confidence of the church where he lives, do not stand in the way of his doing such work as that church may be responsible for. In fact, it may be the duty of his brethren to go farther and to pay him for faithful labor. In fact, I do not see how you could withhold from him a proper remuneration for faithful and judicious labor. But this would not be placing before him the same temptation as to give him credentials and send him forth in the conference as a traveling minister.

"Again I would say, as Mother has said, This is a question which should be submitted to those who have had to deal with his case in the past. Please consider the opinions I have expressed only as suggestive."

At the close of this letter Ellen White personally inscribed the following words of endorsement: "This is correct advice in such cases. Let him walk humbly before God. I see no light in giving him responsibilities."

No more was heard of the matter until early in 1913, when a letter addressed to Mrs. White, dated January 8, 1913, was received from A. L. Miller, the newly-elected president of the Alabama Conference. He wrote:

"Dear Sister White: It becomes my painful duty to write to you concerning the case of Brother William E. Of his past history and life, it is not necessary to write, as you are sufficiently acquainted with the facts, since his case was brought before you by a letter from Elder C. F. McVagh, dated August 15, 1911. I am sorry it becomes necessary to bring this case before you again.

"Elder McVagh's letter was relative to Brother E receiving credentials and becoming a conference laborer.

"The present difficulty is as to whether or not Brother E should be made elder of the Birmingham church, the largest, and now the most influential church in the conference, as the conference headquarters are located in Birmingham. The church is disagreed upon the point in question, and it is having a bad influence upon the work in the city and a more or less deleterious effect throughout the conference. The majority think, because of his capabilities and his late work in the city (as stated in Elder McVagh's letter, a copy of which is herein enclosed), that he should be made elder of the church and act as its pastor, or leader, while others do not favor it because of his life record, and also think that those who have dealt with him in the past should give counsel, and advise as to his becoming elder of the church.

"The counsel given by brethren acquainted with him, and by a recent action of the Southern Union Conference Committee, is that he be not made elder of the church.

"On December 28, Elder S. E. Wight [new president of the Southern Union Conference] held a meeting with the church, at which the question was quite freely discussed. Elder Wight dealt very carefully and cautiously with the case and spoke of Brother E's good traits and qualifications, but let the church know that neither he nor I could feel free to ordain him because of the advice given by those who know him.

"The only point upon which we all could agree was to place his case before the servant of the Lord, and whatever the Lord says, we have all agreed to stand by.

"Personally, none of us have aught to say against Brother E, but love and fellowship him as a brother in the church and so regard him. The church, with Elder Wight as chairman, asked that I place this matter before you and see what instruction the Lord has for us.

"Awaiting an early reply, I am

Sincerely your brother in Christ,
(Signed) A. L. Miller
1700 North Seventh Avenue
Birmingham, Alabama

"P. S. This letter was read to the church, and accepted."

Feeling that his personal appearance before Mrs. White might gain favorable consideration of his case, Brother E went to St. Helena during the second week in January, but Sister White did not feel free to have an interview with him. He then placed in writing the circumstances of his case, which were addressed to Sister White under date of January 13, 1913. On January 14, Elder Miller's letter of January 8, as well as Brother E's letter of January 13, were placed before Sister White. She made the following statements in connection with their reading:]

I do not think any such questions as that ought to be placed before me. I do not think it is my work to deal with any such things unless the case has been plainly opened before me. There should be brethren in the church who have wisdom who can speak decidedly regarding this case. I cannot understand such things. I do not believe that God wants me to take any such burden upon me. If they cannot settle such things among themselves by prayer and fasting, then let them continue [in] fasting and prayer till they can.

Such things will arise. It will come—that is, they will have these difficult questions, and they have got to learn how to treat them. They have got to have an experience. They must bring these things to the Lord, and believe the Lord will hear their prayer, and give them a sound experience in all these things, but they are not to bring them to me.

[Elder W. C. White read portions of Elder McVagh's letter of August 15, 1911, after which Sister White said further:]

I have had no particular light in regard to his case, therefore I dare not speak positively in regard to it.

He has to show the evidence that God accepts him and to give that evidence so that our brethren can have something tangible to build upon. Let them say, We will give you a chance. We will see whether God accepts your labors or not.

But it is not wise for me to take the responsibility of this case. I cannot take the least responsibility. Those who see his actions day by day should know whether he has proved himself, whether God accepts him.

[After reading the letter of William E, written January 13, 1913, Ellen White said:]

I cannot take responsibility in such matters. The burden of doing so is too great. It might cost me my life. Let those appointed of God to bear the responsibility deal with it in accordance with Christian principles.—Ms 2, 1913.

[In connection with the question as to what was involved in his statement of September 15, 1911, relative to the holding of responsible positions by those who have passed through such sad experiences, Elder W. C. White, early in 1913, wrote as follows:

"It now appears that there is a question in the minds of the brethren as to what was meant by the words, 'Do not cut them off from fellowship; do not forbid their working for Christ in a humble capacity, but do not elevate them to positions of responsibility.'

"My understanding of this at the time it was written and my understanding of it today is that the words, 'Do not elevate them to positions of responsibility' referred to such responsibility and elevation as was in the minds of the brethren when they asked for a restoration of credentials and complete recognition as a minister of the conference. It did not occur to me that this could apply to the leadership of the church. The question of the leadership was not then under consideration."]

36. Appeal to Ministers

Clean Hands and Pure Hearts. We are nearing the judgment, and those who bear the message of warning to the world must have clean hands and pure hearts. They must have a living connection with God. The thoughts must be pure and holy, the soul untainted, the body, soul, and spirit be a pure, clean offering to God, or He will not accept it. . . .

The youth, for misdemeanors of a comparatively light character, are treated with much severity. But when men and women of large experience, who have been considered patterns of piety, are revealed in their true character—unsanctified, unholy, impure in thought, debased in conduct—then it is time for such to be dealt with in a decided manner. The greater forbearance that is exercised toward them has only had, as far as my knowledge extends, the influence to cause them to regard their fornication and adultery as a very light matter; and all their pretense has proved to be like morning dew when the sun shines upon it.

False Shepherds of the Flock. No sooner are they placed in temptation than they reveal their moral defects—that they are not partakers of the divine nature, neither have they escaped the corruption that is in the world through lust, but that they are earthly, sensual, devilish. Satan finds in them something that he can work up into marked iniquity, and he improves his opportunity. And the result is [that] those who claim to be shepherds of the flock are carnally minded, leading the sheep of their care, whose purity, modesty, and virtue they should strictly guard, into licentiousness and lewdness.

Accursed Thing in the Camp. Angels of heaven are looking on with shame and grief and disgust. How can the pure angels of heaven minister unto this class? How can they bring heavenly light into the assemblies where such ministers are advocating the law of God, but breaking that law whenever a favorable opportunity presents itself, living a lie, pursuing an underhanded course, working in secret, nursing their polluted thoughts and inflaming their passions, and then taking advantage of women or men who are tempted, like themselves, to break down all barriers and debase their bodies and pollute their souls? How can they do this thing? How can they have any fear of God before them? How can they have any love for God in their souls? Of what value is their faith in the truth?

Cleanse the camp of this moral corruption, if it takes the highest men in the highest positions. God will not be trifled with. Fornication is in our ranks. I know it, for it has been shown me to be strengthening and extending its pollutions. There is much we will never know, but that which is revealed makes the church responsible and guilty unless they show a determined effort to eradicate the evil. Cleanse the camp, for there is an accursed thing in it.

The words of God to Joshua are: "Neither will I be with you anymore, except ye destroy the accursed from among you. Up, sanctify the people, and say, Sanctify yourselves against tomorrow: for thus saith the Lord God of Israel, There is an accursed thing in the midst of thee, O Israel: thou canst not stand before thine enemies, until ye take away the accursed thing from among you" [Joshua 7:12, 13]. These things are written for our benefit, upon whom the ends of the world are come.

No Real Ground of Hope. I have no real ground of hope for those who have stood as shepherds to the flock, and have for years been borne with by the merciful God, following them with reproof, with warnings, with entreaties, but who have hid their evil ways, and continued in them, thus defying the laws of the God of heaven by practicing fornication. We may leave them to work out their own salvation with fear and trembling, after all has been done to reform them, but in no case entrust to them the guardianship of souls. False shepherds! Oh, can it be that the men who

238 Testimonies on Sexual Behavior

have been engaged in this work for a long time will corrupt their ways before the Lord after great experience and special light?—TM 426-428.

Adulterous Ministers More Guilty than Belshazzar. It is a truth which should make every one of us weep that those living in these last days, upon whom the ends of the world are come, are far more guilty than was Belshazzar. This is possible in many ways.

When men have taken upon themselves the vows of consecration, to devote all their powers to the sacred service of God; when they occupy the position of expositors of Bible truth, and have received the solemn charge; when God and angels are summoned as witnesses to the solemn dedication of soul, body, and spirit to God's service—then shall these men who minister in a most holy office desecrate their God-given powers to unholy purposes? Shall the sacred vessel, whom God is to use for a high and holy work, be dragged from its lofty, controlling sphere to administer to debasing lust?

Definition of a Harlot. Is not this idol worship of the most degrading kind?—the lips uttering praises and adoring a sinful human being, pouring forth expressions of ravishing tenderness and adulation which belong alone to God—the powers given to God in solemn consecration administering to a harlot, for any woman who will allow the addresses of another man than her husband, who will listen to his advances, and whose ears will be pleased with the outpouring of lavish words of affection, of adoration, of endearment, is an adulteress and a harlot.—TM 434, 435.

Right Example by Ministers. Ministers of the gospel would be powerful men if they set the Lord always before them and devoted their time to the study of His adorable character. If they did this, there would be no apostasies, there would be none separated from the conference because they have, by their licentious practices, disgraced the cause of God and put Jesus to an open shame. The powers of every minister of the gospel should be employed to educate the believing churches to receive Christ by faith as their personal Saviour, to take Him into their very lives and make Him their Pattern, to learn of Jesus, believe in Jesus, and exalt Jesus. The minister should himself dwell on the character of Christ. He should ponder the truth, and meditate upon the mysteries of redemption, especially the mediatorial work of Christ for this time.—3SM 187.

37. Counsel to a General Conference President

*Unwise Management of a Difficult Case.** Dear Brother: Your last letter is received, and the questions asked in reference to T and Brother V, I cannot answer further than I have done. I am inclined to the same opinion that I had when I wrote John V. The counsel that I gave him I think was safe, and if my good brethren had acted in concert with that counsel, that he should go to England to labor, I think they would have done that which was pleasing to the Lord. I think matters have now come in bad shape for him. He has been entrusted with responsibilities which will have a tendency to elevate him. And it may be that he is not in as good a condition to go forth to labor in some far-off field as he was months ago.

---

*Extracts from a letter written from Europe to Elder George I. Butler concerning several ministers in the United States who had transgressed the seventh commandment.

I have not changed my mind in his case. I do not think that it has been managed wisely, taking his soul into consideration. He proposed to prove himself, on his own responsibility, without expense to the conference, and he should have had his chance.

Ellen White's Encouraging Dream. In regard to Brother H, I do not think your management the wisest. I think he should have a chance for his life. If the man is willing and desirous of coming to Europe on his own responsibility, perhaps that would be wisdom. He will never recover himself where he is under present circumstances. I did have a dream many months ago, which showed him restored with the blessing of God resting upon him, but he was not brought to this position by the help of yourself or Elder Haskell, but would have as far as you both were concerned, the attitude you assumed toward him, ever remained in the dark, and his light would have gone out in darkness.

That dream prompted the letter that W. C. White wrote him asking him in reference to coming to Europe, which your conference had voted one year ago that he should do, and made a mistake in sending him to Oakland instead of Europe. He should have come here at once.

A Decision in Regard to Counseling. We shall not urge anything more in his case, but shall do the uttermost in our power to save his soul from death, and hide a multitude of sins. I am in great perplexity at times, and have about come to the conclusion when a case of error and grievous sin is presented before me, to say nothing to my ministering brethren if they do not know the matter themselves, but labor earnestly for the erring one, and encourage him to hope in God's mercy and cling to the merits of a crucified and risen Saviour, look to the Lamb of God in repentance and contrition, and live in His strength. "Come now, and let us reason together; . . . though your sins be as scarlet, they shall be as white as snow; though they be red like crimson, they shall be as wool'' [Isa. 1:18].

There is not the mingling of the elements of character that brings justice and mercy and the love of God into beautiful harmony. There is altogether too much talking, too many strong words and feelings that the Lord has nothing to do with, and these strong feelings influence our good brethren.

Compassion and Sympathy, But Also Plain Dealing. I am compelled to deal plainly and rebuke sin, and then I have it in my heart, placed there by the Spirit of Christ, to labor in faith, in tender sympathy and compassion for the erring. I will not let them alone; I will not leave them to become the sport of Satan's temptations. I will not myself act the part of the adversary of souls, as is represented by Joshua and the Angel. Souls cost the price of my Redeemer's blood.

When men, themselves liable to temptation, erring mortals, shall be free to pronounce upon another's case, who is humbled in the dust, and shall take it on themselves to decide by their own feelings or the feelings of their brethren, just how much feeling the erring one should manifest to be pardoned, [they are] taking on themselves that which God has not required of them. When I know that there are those who have fallen into great sin, but we have labored with and for them, and God has afterwards accepted their labors, when these have pleaded for me to let them go and not to burden myself for them, I have said, ''I will not give you up; you must gather strength to overcome.'' These men are now in active service. . . .

No Sanction of Sin, But the Winning of Sinners. My mind is greatly perplexed over these things, because I cannot harmonize them with the course that is being pursued. I am fearful to sanction sin, and I am fearful to let go of the sinner and make no effort to restore him. I think that if our hearts were more fully imbued with the Spirit of Christ, we should have His melting love, and should work with spiritual power to restore the erring and not leave them under Satan's control.

Need of Good Heart Religion. We need good heart religion, that we shall not only reprove, rebuke, exhort with all long-suffering and doctrine, but we shall take the erring in our arms of faith and bear them to the cross of Christ. We must bring them in contact with the sin-pardoning Saviour.

I am more pained than I can express to see so little aptitude and skill to save souls that are ensnared by Satan. I see such a cold Phariseeism, holding off at arm's length the one who has been deluded by the adversary of souls, and then I think: What if Jesus treated us in this way? Is this spirit to grow among us? If so, my brethren must excuse me; I cannot labor with them. I will not be a party to this kind of labor.

Hearts of Flesh, Not Hearts of Iron. I call to mind the shepherd hunting the lost sheep and the prodigal son. I want those parables to have their influence upon my heart and my mind. I think of Jesus, what love and tenderness He manifested for erring, fallen man, and then I think of the severe judgment one pronounces upon his brother who has failed under temptation, and my heart becomes sick. I see the iron in hearts, and think we should pray for hearts of flesh. . . .

I wish that we had much more of the Spirit of Christ and a great deal less self, and less of human opinions. If we err, let it be on the side of mercy rather than on the side of condemnation and harsh dealing.—Letter 16, 1887.

38. Counsels to City Mission and Institutional Leaders

*Conduct of City Mission Leaders.** Missions are essential as the foundation of missionary effort in our cities; but unless those standing at the head of these missions make strenuous efforts to guard every post, so that Satan shall not control, losses will be sustained. . . .

There should be connected with the mission, married persons who will conduct themselves with the strictest propriety. But the danger is not alone from youth, but from married men and women; workers must build up the walls of modesty and virtue about themselves so that women will not allure men, and men will not allure women from strict propriety. Abstain from even the very appearance of evil.

Love-sick sentimentalism prevails. Married men receive attention from married or unmarried women; women also appear to be charmed, and lose reason and spiritual discernment and good common sense; they do the very things that the Word of God condemns. . . . Warnings and reproofs are before them in clear lines, yet they go over the same path that others have traveled before them. It is like an infatuating game which they are playing. Satan leads them on to ruin themselves, to imperil the cause of God, to crucify the Son of God afresh, and put Him to an open shame.

There is no safety for any man, young or old, unless he feels the necessity of seeking counsel of God at every step. Those only who maintain a close communion with God will learn to place His estimate upon men, to reverence the pure, the good, the humble, the meek. The heart must be gar-

---

*This counsel was given in 1893, when "city mission" was a name for a particular form of evangelistic endeavor. It consisted of a team composed of ministers, colporteurs, nurses, and others. Today it is sometimes called a "field school."

risoned as was that of Joseph. Then temptations to depart from integrity will be met with decision. "How can I do this great wickedness and sin against God?" The strongest temptation is no excuse for sin. No matter how severe the pressure brought to bear upon you, sin is your own act. The seat of the difficulty is the unrenewed heart.

The Worst Kind of Traitor. A man who claims to have believed present truth for years, and is counted worthy by his brethren to fill positions of trust in missions or in our institutions, may become careless when a change of circumstances brings him into temptations, and in time he may tempt others. His case is sad indeed, for he reveals the workings of a corrupt heart, a want of that principle which every Christian should possess.

When one who is entrusted with great responsibilities betrays his sacred trust and gives himself into the hands of Satan as an instrument of unrighteousness to sow the seeds of evil, corrupting the hearts and minds of others, he is a traitor of the worst type. From one such tainted, polluted mind the youth often receive the first impure thoughts that lead to a life of shame and defilement.

Workers Lacking in Firm Principle. If men placed at the head of a mission have not firmness of principle that will preserve them from every vestige of commonness and unbecoming familiarity with young girls and women, after the light which has been so plainly given, let them be discharged without a second trial. There is a depravity of the soul which leads to these careless habits and practices, which will far overbalance all the good such persons can do. We are living in an age of moral debasement; the world is as a second Sodom. Those who look for the coming of the Son of man, those who know that they are right upon the borders of the eternal world, should set an example in harmony with their faith. Those who do not maintain purity and holiness are not accepted of God. The true children of God have deep-rooted principles which will not be moved by temptations, because Christ is abiding in their hearts by faith.

A Second Trial Useless. A second trial would be of no avail to those whose moral sense is so perverted that they cannot see their danger. If after they have long held the truth, [if] its sanctifying power has not established the character in piety, virtue, and purity, let them be disconnected from the missions without delay, for through these Satan will insinuate the same lax sentiments in the minds of those who ought to have an example of virtue and moral dignity. Anything that approaches love-sick sentimentalism, any imitation of commonness, should be decidedly rebuked.—GCB 1893, p. 162.

No Time for Corrupt Impulses. Our probation is short at best. We have no time to spend in indulging corrupt impulses. The familiarity of married men with married women and young girls is disgusting in the sight of God and holy angels. The forwardness of young girls in placing themselves in the company of young men, hanging around where they are at work, entering into conversation with them, talking common, idle talk, is belittling to womanhood. It lowers them, even in the estimation of those who themselves do such things.

There is a positive necessity for reform in all our institutions. All frivolity, all undue attention of men and women, must be condemned and discontinued. Some, even married men, who have indulged in this trifling familiarity, have endeavored to excuse themselves and escape censure by claiming that they have done no moral wrong. Was it no moral wrong to jest, joke, and pay flattering attentions to young women? Are you not starting in their minds a a train of thought which it is impossible for you to change? Do you not by your levity and coquetry, sanction such conduct?

You who hold positions of trust, and claim to be Christians, do you not give countenance to a familiarity which leads to sin? What record is made in the books of heaven by the divine Watcher? Was there no moral wrong done to the souls of those with whom you were so familiar? Indeed there was. Impressions were made that will be enduring. These girls are confirmed in coquetry and flirting. Every such indulgence tends to make them coarse and bold. They become more and more infatuated with the society of men and women who are trifling and frivolous, whose conversation is anything but holy, pure, and ennobling.

Definition of Moral Wrong. "No moral wrong." This has been the excuse made by everyone reproved for similar conduct. What is moral wrong? Have your spiritual senses become so blinded that you cannot discern the truth? Do you not know that grapevines will not bear thorns, nor a bramble bush grapes? If the truth is brought into the inner sanctuary of the soul, it will create a pure moral taste. Then all these objectionable, demoralizing practices will be seen to be a positive denial of Christ, a sin which will pollute the soul. . . . All trifling, jesting, joking, and flattery spoken to young girls or women, boys or men, are thornberries, and that which produces them is a thornbush, for the tree is known by its fruits.

Let not those who profess the religion of Christ descend to trifling conversation, to unbecoming familiarity with women of any class, married or single. They should keep their proper places with all dignity. At the same time they may be sociable, kind, and courteous to all.

Young ladies should be reserved and modest. When they walk out, if in health, they do not need the supporting arm of any man. They should give no occasion for their good to be evil spoken of.

Every Health Institution a Missionary Field. Men should be chosen to stand at the head of our institutions who have not only good, sound judgment, but who have a high moral tone, who will be circumspect in their deportment, pure in speech, remembering their high and holy calling and that there is a Watcher, a true witness to every word and act. If men in our institutions exhibit a low grade of thought, if their conversation tends to corrupt rather than elevate, let them be removed at once from any connection with the institution, for they will surely demoralize others. The well-being of the entire institution is to be maintained. Ever bear in mind that each of our health institutions is a missionary field. God's eye is upon it day and night. No one should feel at liberty to allow even the appearance of evil.—SpT Series B, No. 16, pp. 6, 7.

39. The Adulterer and Church Membership

An Early Ellen White Statement. The Lord gave us labor of spirit last first day [Sunday, February 5, 1854], and while we were engaged in earnest prayer I was taken off in vision and saw the state of some of the professed Israel of God. I saw the situation of many at our meeting in Oswego. I saw that they were standing in the way of the work of God, especially those at Caughdenoy. I saw that God's frown was upon them, also upon some in Roosevelt.

Said the angel, "The ax has not been laid at the root of the tree." Those who have indulged in the wicked passions of the heart have been fellowshiped. If God had made Brother Roosevelt an overseer of the flock, he would have seen the evil and corruption among the people. The ax has not been laid at the root of the tree. God has not altered nor changed. He is a jealous God, and will not look upon sin now with any more allowance than He did among ancient Israel. Sin is sin. Sins have not been held forth in their sinfulness, but it has been made to appear as though sins have been lightly regarded by God.

An Enormous Sin. I saw that the seventh commandment has been violated by some who are now held in fellowship by the church. This has brought God's frown upon them. This sin is awful in these last days, but the church [members] have brought God's frown and curse upon them by regarding the sin so lightly. I saw it was an enormous sin and there have not been as vigilant efforts made as there should have been to satisfy the displeasure of God and remove His frown by taking a strict, thorough course with the offender.

It has had an awful, corrupting influence upon the young. They see how lightly the sin of breaking the seventh commandment is regarded, and the one who commits this horrid sin thinks that all he has to do is to confess that he was wrong and is sorry, and he is then to have all the privileges of the house of God and be held in [the] embrace or fellowship of the church.

They have thought it was not so great a sin, but have lightly esteemed the breaking of the seventh commandment. This has been sufficient to remove the ark of God from the camp, if there were no other sins to cause the ark to be taken away and weaken Israel.

Suspension From the Church for Adulterers. Those who break the seventh commandment should be suspended from the church, and not have its fellowship nor the privileges of the house of God. Said the angel, "This is not a sin of ignorance. It is a knowing sin and will receive the awful visitation of God, whether he who commits it be old or young.''

High-handed, Deliberate Sinning. Never was this sin regarded by God as being so exceedingly sinful as at the present time. Why? Because God is purifying unto Himself a peculiar people, zealous of good works. It is at the very time when God is purifying this peculiar people unto Himself that [unsanctified] individuals step in among us. Notwithstanding the straight truths they have heard—the terrors of the Word of God set before them, and all the blazing truth for these last days calculated to arouse Israel—they sin with a high hand, give way to all the loose passions of the carnal heart, gratify their animal propensities, disgrace the cause of God, and then confess they have sinned and are sorry!

And the church receives them and says "Amen" to their prayers and exhortations, which are a stink in the nostrils of God, and cause His wrath to come upon the camp. He will not dwell in their assemblies. Those who move on thus heedlessly, plastering over these sins, will be left to their own ways, to be filled with their own doings.

Those who anciently committed these sins were taken without the camp and stoned to death. Temporal and eternal death was their doom; and because the penalty of stoning to death is abolished, this sin is indulged in beyond measure and is thought to be a small offense.—Ms 3, 1854.

*No Help for This Man.** It is impossible for E to be fellowshiped by the church of God. He has placed himself

---

*The White Estate has no firm documentation on the nature of E's transgression, but Arthur L. White recalls hearing his father, W. C. White, refer to it as a particularly revolting case of incest.

where he cannot be helped by the church, where he can have no communion with, nor voice in, the church. He has placed himself there in the face of light and truth. He has stubbornly chosen his own course, and refused to listen to reproof. He has followed the inclinations of his corrupt heart, has violated the holy law of God, and has disgraced the cause of present truth.

If he repents ever so heartily, the church must let his case alone. If he goes to heaven, it must be alone, without the fellowship of the church. A standing rebuke from God and the church must ever rest upon him that the standard of morality be not lowered to the very dust.—1T 215.

40. A Statement by Ellen and James White *

Possibility of Restoration. In regard to the case of the injured Sister A. G., we would say in reply to the questions of J.H.W., that it is a feature in the cases of most who have been overtaken in sin, as her husband has, that they have no real sense of their villainy. Some, however, do, and are restored to the church, but not till they have merited the confidence of the people of God by unqualified confessions, and a period of sincere repentance. This case presents difficulties not found in some, and we would add only the following:

1. In cases of the violation of the seventh commandment, where the guilty party does not manifest true repentance, if the injured party can obtain a divorce without making their own cases and that of their children, if they have them, worse by so doing, they should be free.

---

*Inasmuch as this statement was issued jointly by James and Ellen White, it seems clear that the views expressed had the full sanction of Ellen White.

2. If they would be liable to place themselves and their children in worse condition by a divorce, we know of no scripture that would make the innocent party guilty by remaining.

3. Time, and labor, and prayer, and patience, and faith, and a godly life, might work a reform. To live with one who has broken the marriage vows, and is covered all over with the disgrace and shame of guilty love, and realizes it not, is an eating canker to the soul; and yet, a divorce is a lifelong, heartfelt sore. God pity the innocent party. Marriage should be considered well before contracted.

4. Why! oh why! will men and women who might be respectable, and good, and reach heaven at last, sell themselves to the devil so cheap, wound their bosom friends, disgrace their families, bring a reproach upon the cause, and go to hell at last? God have mercy. Why will not those who are overtaken in crime manifest repentance proportionate to the enormity of their crime, and fly to Christ for mercy, and heal, as far as possible, the wounds they have made?

5. But, if they will not do as they should, and if the innocent have forfeited the legal right to a divorce by living with the guilty after his guilt is known, we do not see that sin rests upon the innocent in remaining, and her moral right in departing seems questionable if her health and life be not greatly endangered in so remaining.

6. As in the days of Noah, one of the signs of these times is a passion for injudicious and hasty marriages. Satan is in this. If Paul could remain single, and recommend the same to others, that he and they might be wholly the Lord's, why not those who would be wholly His, and wish to make a sure thing of avoiding the cares, trials, and bitter anguish so frequent in the experiences of those who choose the married life, remain as he was? And more, if he chose to remain so,

and could recommend it to others, eighteen centuries since, would not to remain as he was be a commendable course for those who are waiting for the coming of the Son of man, unless evidences were unquestionable that they were bettering their condition, and making heaven more sure by so doing? When so much is at stake, why not be on the sure side every time?—RH March 24, 1868.

Section X

LOVE FOR THE ERRING AND TEMPTED

41. God's Love for the Sinner

Heaven and the Heart of Man. While Christ opens heaven to man, the life which He imparts opens the heart of man to heaven. Sin not only shuts us away from God, but destroys in the human soul the desire and the capacity for knowing Him. All this work of evil it is Christ's mission to undo. The faculties of the soul, paralyzed by sin, the darkened mind, the perverted will, He has power to invigorate and to restore. He opens to us the riches of the universe, and by Him the power to discern and to appropriate these treasures is imparted.—Ed 28, 29.

Each Individual Known by Jesus. Jesus knows us individually, and is touched with the feeling of our infirmities. He knows us all by name. He knows the very house in which we live, the name of each occupant. He has at times given directions to His servants to go to a certain street in a certain city, to such a house, to find one of His sheep.

Every soul is as fully known to Jesus as if he were the only one for whom the Saviour died. The distress of every one touches His heart. The cry for aid reaches His ear. He came to draw all men unto Himself. He bids them, "Follow Me," and His Spirit moves upon their hearts to draw them to come to Him. Many refuse to be drawn. Jesus knows

(253)

who they are. He also knows who gladly hear His call, and are ready to come under His pastoral care. He says, "My sheep hear My voice, and I know them, and they follow Me." He cares for each one as if there were not another on the face of the earth.—DA 479, 480.

Rebuke of Devil Possession Seven Times. Mary had been looked upon as a great sinner, but Christ knew the circumstances that had shaped her life. He might have extinguished every spark of hope in her soul, but He did not. It was He who had lifted her from despair and ruin. Seven times she had heard His rebuke of the demons that controlled her heart and mind. She had heard His strong cries to the Father in her behalf. She knew how offensive is sin to His unsullied purity, and in His strength she had overcome.

The Transformation of Mary. When to human eyes her case appeared hopeless, Christ saw in Mary capabilities for good. He saw the better traits of her character. The plan of redemption has invested humanity with great possibilities, and in Mary these possibilities were to be realized. Through His grace she became a partaker of the divine nature. The one who had fallen, and whose mind had been a habitation of demons, was brought very near to the Saviour in fellowship and ministry.

It was Mary who sat at His feet and learned of Him. It was Mary who poured upon His head the precious anointing oil, and bathed His feet with her tears. Mary stood beside the cross, and followed Him to the sepulcher. Mary was first at the tomb after His resurrection. It was Mary who first proclaimed a risen Saviour.

The Greater the Sin, the Greater the Need for Jesus. Jesus knows the circumstances of every soul. You may say, I am sinful, very sinful. You may be, but the worse you are, the more you need Jesus. He turns no weeping, contrite one away. He does not tell to any all that He might reveal, but He bids every trembling soul take courage. Freely will He pardon all who come to Him for forgiveness and restoration.

Christ might commission the angels of heaven to pour out the vials of His wrath on our world, to destroy those who are filled with hatred of God. He might wipe this dark spot from His universe, but He does not do this. He is today standing at the altar of incense, presenting before God the prayers of those who desire His help.

The souls that turn to Him for refuge, Jesus lifts above the accusing and the strife of tongues. No man or evil angel can impeach these souls. Christ unites them to His own divine-human nature. They stand beside the great Sin Bearer in the light proceeding from the throne of God. ''Who shall lay anything to the charge of God's elect? It is God that justifieth. Who is he that condemneth? It is Christ that died, yea rather, that is risen again, who is even at the right hand of God, who also maketh intercession for us'' [Rom. 8:33, 34].—DA 568.

A Never-failing Helper. The soul that has given himself to Christ is more precious in His sight than the whole world. The Saviour would have passed through the agony of Calvary that one might be saved in His kingdom. He will never abandon one for whom He has died. Unless His followers choose to leave Him, He will hold them fast.

Through all our trials we have a never-failing Helper. He does not leave us alone to struggle with temptation, to battle with evil, and be finally crushed with burdens and sorrow. Though now He is hidden from mortal sight, the ear of faith can hear His voice saying, Fear not; I am with you. ''I

am He that liveth, and was dead; and, behold, I am alive
forevermore'' [Rev. 1:18]. I have endured your sorrows, experienced your struggles, encountered your temptations. I
know your tears; I also have wept. The griefs that lie too
deep to be breathed into any human ear, I know. Think not
that you are desolate and forsaken. Though your pain touch
no responsive chord in any heart on earth, look unto Me,
and live. ''The mountains shall depart, and the hills be
removed; but My kindness shall not depart from thee,
neither shall the covenant of My peace be removed, saith
the Lord that hath mercy on thee'' (Isa. 54:10).—DA 483.

Hatred of Sin, Love for Sinners. Jesus arose, and looking
at the woman said, ''Woman, where are those thine accusers? hath no man condemned thee? She said, No man,
Lord. And Jesus said unto her, Neither do I condemn thee:
go, and sin no more.''

The woman had stood before Jesus, cowering with fear.
His words, ''He that is without sin among you, let him first
cast a stone,'' had come to her as a death sentence. She
dared not lift her eyes to the Saviour's face, but silently
awaited her doom. In astonishment she saw her accusers
depart speechless and confounded; then those words of
hope fell upon her ear, ''Neither do I condemn thee: go, and
sin no more.'' Her heart was melted, and she cast herself at
the feet of Jesus, sobbing out her grateful love, and with bitter tears confessing her sins.

Beginning of a New Life. This was to her the beginning
of a new life, a life of purity and peace, devoted to the
service of God. In the uplifting of this fallen soul, Jesus
performed a greater miracle than in healing the most
grievous physical disease; He cured the spiritual malady
which is unto death everlasting. This penitent woman be-

came one of His most steadfast followers. With self-sacrificing love and devotion she repaid His forgiving mercy.

In His act of pardoning this woman and encouraging her to live a better life, the character of Jesus shines forth in the beauty of perfect righteousness. While He does not palliate sin, nor lessen the sense of guilt, He seeks not to condemn, but to save. The world had for this erring woman only contempt and scorn, but Jesus speaks words of comfort and hope. The Sinless One pities the weakness of the sinner and reaches to her a helping hand. While the hypocritical Pharisees denounce, Jesus bids her, "Go, and sin no more."

Christian Love Slow of Censure. It is not Christ's follower that, with averted eyes, turns from the erring, leaving them unhindered to pursue their downward course. Those who are forward in accusing others, and zealous in bringing them to justice, are often in their own lives more guilty than they. Men hate the sinner, while they love the sin. Christ hates the sin, but loves the sinner. This will be the spirit of all who follow Him. Christian love is slow to censure, quick to discern penitence, ready to forgive, to encourage, to set the wanderer in the path of holiness, and to stay his feet therein.—DA 461, 462.

Jesus, Friend of Sinners. I would call your attention to the precious promises in the Word of God. Not all who are children of God have the same powers, the same temperaments, the same confidence and boldness. I am glad indeed that our feelings are no evidence that we are not children of God. The enemy will tempt you to think that you have done things that have separated you from God and that He no longer loves you, but our Lord loves us still, and we may know by the words He has placed on record for just such cases as yours. "If any man sin, we have an advocate with the Father, Jesus Christ the righteous" [1 John 2:1]. "If we confess our sins, He is faithful and just to forgive us our sins, and to cleanse us from all unrighteousness" [1 John 1:9].

Now, my dear sister, I have evidence that God loves you; and the precious Saviour, who gave Himself for you, will not thrust you from Him because you are tempted, and in your weakness may have been overcome. He loves you still.

Peter denied his Lord in the hour of trial, but Jesus did not forsake His poor disciple. Although Peter hated himself, the Lord loved him, and after His resurrection He called him by name and sent him a loving message. Oh, what a kind, loving, compassionate Saviour we have! And He loves us though we err.

Sweet Promises of God. Now, do not worry yourself out of the arms of the dear Saviour, but rest trustingly in faith. He loves you; He cares for you. He is blessing you, and will give you His peace and grace. He is saying to you, "Thy sins be forgiven thee" [Matt. 9:2]. You may be depressed with bodily infirmities, but that is not evidence that the Lord is not working in your behalf every day. He will pardon you, and that abundantly. Gather to your soul the sweet promises of God. Jesus is our constant, unfailing Friend, and He wants you to trust in Him.

God is at work, and Satan also is at work. Satan would have our minds drawn away from the mighty Helper, to ponder over our degradation of soul, and feel that all its powers are being wasted and God dishonored. Look away from yourself to the perfection of Christ.

Christ's Righteousness for Us. We cannot manufacture a righteousness for ourselves. Christ has in His hands the pure robes of righteousness, and He will put them upon us. He will speak sweet words of forgiveness and promise. He presents to our thirsty souls fountains of living water whereby we may be refreshed. He bids us come unto Him with all our burdens, all our griefs, and He says we shall find rest. Therefore, if we come to Him, we must believe that He speaks pardon, and we must show our faith by resting in His love. The heart is moved by all that is tender and pure and lofty—high ambition, holy joys, ennobling motives, endearing sympathies, and needful help.

Offer of Free Pardon. Jesus sees the guilt of the past, and speaks pardon, and we must not dishonor Him by doubting His love. This feeling of guiltiness must be laid at the foot of the cross of Calvary. The sense of sinfulness has poisoned the springs of life and of true happiness. Now Jesus says, "Lay it all on Me. I will take your sins. I will give you peace. Banish no longer your self-respect, for I have bought you with the price of My own blood. You are Mine. Your weakened will I will strengthen; your remorse for sin I will remove."

Then turn your grateful heart, trembling with uncertainty, to Him and lay hold on the hope set before you. God accepts your broken, contrite heart, and extends to you free pardon. He offers to adopt you into His family, with His grace to help your weakness. And the dear Saviour will lead you on step by step, you placing your hand in His, and letting Him guide you.

Search for the precious promises of God. If Satan thrusts threatenings before your mind, turn from them, and cling to the promises, and let your soul be comforted by their brightness. The cloud is dark in itself, but when filled with the light, it is turned to the brightness of gold, for the glory of God is upon it.

May the Lord bless to your soul these few words He has prompted me to write.—Letter 99, 1896.

Objects of God's Loving Interest. The Lord God through Jesus Christ holds out His hand all the day long in invitation to the sinful and fallen. He will receive all. He welcomes all. It is His glory to pardon the chief of sinners. He will take the prey from the mighty, He will deliver the captive, He will pluck the brand from the burning. He will lower the golden chain of His mercy to the lowest depth of human wretchedness, and lift up the debased soul contaminated with sin.

Every human being is the object of loving interest to Him who gave His life that He might bring men back to God. Souls guilty and helpless, liable to be destroyed by the arts and snares of Satan, are cared for as a shepherd cares for the sheep of his flock.—MH 161, 162.

42. Understanding Others

Heart Trials of One With Remorse. When one at fault becomes conscious of his error, be careful not to destroy his self-respect. Do not discourage him by indifference or distrust. Do not say, "Before giving him my confidence, I will wait to see whether he will hold out." Often this very distrust causes the tempted one to stumble.

We should strive to understand the weakness of others. We know little of the heart trials of those who have been bound in chains of darkness and who lack resolution and moral power. Most pitiable is the condition of him who is suffering under remorse; he is as one stunned, staggering, sinking into the dust. He can see nothing clearly. The mind is beclouded, he knows not what steps to take. Many a poor soul is misunderstood, unappreciated, full of distress and agony—a lost, straying sheep. He cannot find God, yet he has an intense longing for pardon and peace.

Powerful Influences Toward Evil. Oh, let no word be spoken to cause deeper pain! To the soul weary of a life of sin, but knowing not where to find relief, present the compassionate Saviour. Take him by the hand, lift him up, speak to him words of courage and hope. Help him to grasp the hand of the Saviour. . . . We need to put ourselves in the place of the tempted ones. Consider the power of heredity, the influence of evil associations and surroundings, the power of wrong habits. Can we wonder that under such influences many become degraded? Can we wonder that they should be slow to respond to efforts for their uplifting?—MH 167, 168.

Tender Sympathy. Wondrous love, that God, the infinite God, has made it our privilege to approach Him by the endearing name of "Father"! No earthly parent could plead more earnestly with an erring child than He who has made us pleads with the transgressor. No human interest has ever followed the impenitent with such tender invitations.

Then with what tender sympathy should we labor for those who are erring and sinful, who are perishing around us. We must work in the spirit in which Christ worked, in the compassionate tenderness that He manifested. When we shall, by living faith, claim the promises of God, when we shall live by every word that proceedeth out of the mouth of God, we place ourselves on the side of Christ, and we have His Spirit and His grace to work with our efforts to bring souls to a knowledge of the divine will.—Ms 35, 1886.

Compassion for the Guilty. How little do we enter into sympathy with Christ on that which should be the strongest bond of union between us and Him—compassion for depraved, guilty, suffering souls, dead in trespasses and sins! The inhumanity of man toward man is our greatest sin. Many think that they are representing the justice of God while they wholly fail of representing His tenderness and His great love. Often the ones whom they meet with sternness and severity are under the stress of temptation. Satan is wrestling with these souls, and harsh, unsympathetic words discourage them and cause them to fall a prey to the tempter's power.

It is a delicate matter to deal with minds. Only He who reads the heart knows how to bring men to repentance. Only His wisdom can give us success in reaching the lost. You may stand up stiffly, feeling, "I am holier than thou," and it matters not how correct your reasoning or how true your words; they will never touch hearts. The love of Christ, manifested in word and act, will win its way to the soul, when the reiteration of precept or argument would accomplish nothing.

We need more of Christlike sympathy, not merely sympathy for those who appear to us to be faultless, but sympathy for poor, suffering, struggling souls, who are often overtaken in fault, sinning and repenting, tempted and discouraged. We are to go to our fellow men, touched, like our merciful High Priest, with the feeling of their infirmities.— MH 163, 164.

Result of Coldness and Neglect. But there has been among us as a people a lack of deep, earnest, soul-touching sympathy and love for the tempted and the erring. Many have manifested great coldness and sinful neglect, represented by Christ as passing by on the other side, keeping as far as possible from those who most need help. The newly converted soul often has fierce conflicts with established habits or with some special form of temptation, and, being overcome by some master passion or tendency, he is guilty of indiscretion or actual wrong. It is then that energy, tact, and wisdom are required of his brethren, that he may be restored to spiritual health. In such cases the instructions of God's Word apply: "Brethren, if a man be overtaken in a fault, ye which are spiritual, restore such an one in a spirit of meekness; considering thyself, lest thou also be tempted." "We then that are strong ought to bear the infirmities of the weak, and not to please ourselves."

But how little of the pitying tenderness of Christ is manifested by His professed followers! When one errs, others too often feel at liberty to make the case appear as bad as possible. Those who perhaps are guilty of fully as great sins in some other direction, will treat their brother with cruel severity. Errors committed through ignorance, thoughtlessness, or weakness are exaggerated into willful, premeditated sin. As they see souls going astray, some fold their hands and say, "I told you so. I knew there was no dependence to be placed upon them." Thus they place themselves in the attitude of Satan, exulting in spirit that their evil surmisings have proved to be correct.—5T 604, 605.

Love for the Erring. We are not all organized alike, and many have not been educated aright. Their education has been deficient. Some have had a quick temper transmitted to them, and their education in childhood has not taught them self-control. With this fiery temper, envy and jealousy are frequently united. Others are faulty in other respects. Some are dishonest in deal, overreaching in trade. Others are arbitrary in their families, loving to rule. Their lives are far from being correct. Their education was all wrong. They were not told the sin of yielding to the control of these evil traits; therefore sin does not appear to them so exceedingly sinful. Others, whose education has not been so faulty, who have had better training, have developed a much less objectionable character. The Christian life of all is very much affected for good or for evil by their previous education.

Jesus, our Advocate, is acquainted with all the circumstances with which we are surrounded and deals with us according to the light we have had and the circumstances in which we are placed. Some have a much better organization than others. While some are continually harassed, afflicted, and in trouble because of their unhappy traits of character, having to war with internal foes and the corruption of their nature, others have not half so much to battle against. They pass along almost free from the difficulties which their brethren and sisters who are not so favorably organized are laboring under.—2T 74.

Welcome for the Repentant. "And of some have compassion, making a difference" [Jude 22]. Those who are wise in the wisdom born of God will see souls in need of help, souls who have been overcome, and who, though they have sincerely repented, would scarcely dare, without encouragement, to lay hold of hope. The Lord will put it into the hearts of those who are stewards of His grace to welcome these trembling, repentant souls to their loving fellowship. His true followers will not treat sinners as if they were beyond forgiveness. They will have compassion on those whose circumstances have been unfavorable, and who have allowed Satan to lead them in forbidden paths.

These souls have sinned against God, but if they repent and show the genuineness of their repentance by earnest efforts to serve the Lord, who shall dare forbid them? Encourage them. Give them an opportunity to regain what they have lost. Pride, covetousness, sensuality, may have been their besetting sins. Point out their errors, but not in a way that will drive them from Christ. By words of loving compassion draw them to Him. However low they may have fallen, do not destroy their hope of pardon. Labor for them, pray with them, point them to the Redeemer. . . .

No Condemnation of Others. By earnest, Christlike efforts, men will be convicted and converted, and God will speak pardon to them. Let no one turn away a soul who leaves the service of Satan and asks Jesus for pardon. "Of some have compassion, making a difference." When they give evidence that the Spirit of God is striving with them, present to them every encouragement for entering the Lord's service. Do not discourage them by indifference, by drawing away from them with an air of, "I am holier than thou" [Isa. 65:5].

Those who act as Pharisees may not be guilty of exactly the same sins they condemn in others, but they may be guilty of sins much greater in the sight of God. Each will be rewarded according to his work. Let those who condemn others take heed to themselves, lest they be condemned by God for Phariseeism.—Ms 37, 1902.

People With Love, Not Like Chestnut Burs. We must expect to meet and bear with great imperfections in those who are young and inexperienced. Christ has bidden us seek to restore such in the spirit of meekness, and He holds us responsible for [wrongly] pursuing a course which will drive them to discouragement, despair, and ruin. Unless we daily cultivate the precious plant of love we are in danger of becoming narrow, unsympathetic, bigoted, and critical, esteeming ourselves righteous when we are far from being approved of God. Some are uncourteous, abrupt, and harsh. They are like chestnut burs—they prick whenever touched. These do incalculable harm by misrepresenting our loving Saviour.

We must come up to a higher standard, or we are unworthy of the Christian name. We should cultivate the spirit with which Christ labored to save the erring. They are as dear to Him as we are. They are equally capable of being trophies of His grace and heirs of the kingdom. But they are exposed to the snares of a wily foe, exposed to danger and defilement, and without the saving grace of Christ, to certain ruin. Did we view this matter in the right light, how would our zeal be quickened and our earnest, self-sacrificing efforts be multiplied, that we might come close to those who need our help, our prayers, our sympathy, and our love!—5T 605, 606.

Jesus, Our Example. It was the outcast, the publican and sinner, the despised of the nations, that Christ called and by His loving-kindness compelled to come unto Him. The one class that He would never countenance was those who stood apart in their self-esteem and looked down upon others. . . .

Even those who had fallen the lowest He treated with respect. It was continual pain to Christ to be brought into contact with enmity, depravity, and impurity; but never did He utter one expression to show that His sensibilities were shocked or His refined tastes offended. Whatever the evil habits, the strong prejudices, or the overbearing passions of human beings, He met them all with pitying tenderness. As we partake of His Spirit, we shall regard all men as brethren, with similar temptations and trials, often falling and struggling to rise again, battling with discouragements and difficulties, craving sympathy and help. Then we shall meet them in such a way as not to discourage or repel them, but to awaken hope in their hearts.—MH 164, 165.

Appendix A

MASTURBATION AND INSANITY

In his scholarly study on "Masturbatory Insanity; The History of an Idea," (*Journal of Mental Science* 108:1, Jan., 1962), E. H. Hare refers to a study of 500 patients admitted consecutively to the Iowa State Psychopathic Hospital. He states that the authors of the study (Malamud, W., and Palmer, G., "The Role Played by Masturbation in the Causation of Mental Disturbances, *Journal of Nervous and Mental Disorders*, 76:220, 1932) found that in twenty-two cases masturbation was "apparently the most important cause of disorder."

He then continues:

"The authors concluded that it was the mental conflict engendered by masturbation rather than the habit itself which led to the illness, and they believed this conclusion to be supported by the efficacy of psychotherapy directed towards readjusting the patient's ideas about masturbation. Yet the fact that fifteen of the twenty-two patients suffered from depression must raise doubts about the validity even of this temperate conclusion, for the depressed patient is not only prone to blame himself for neglect of what he believes to be the rules of health, but also tends to recover from his illness whether treated by psychotherapy or not."—p. 22.

Thus Hare questions the conclusions of Malamud and Palmer, but says, significantly, that their study is "one of the very few attempts (indeed, as far as my reading goes, the only real attempt) at a scientific study of the masturbatory hypothesis [the hypothesis that masturbation can cause insanity]."

After acknowledging that "there is no way of disproving the masturbatory hypothesis," Hare offers his final conclusion: "All we can say, from the evidence, is that the association between masturbation and mental disorder is weak and inconstant and that therefore, if masturbation is a causal factor, it is probably not a very important one" (*Ibid.* p. 19).

So, although this authority minimizes the possibility that masturbation and insanity might be linked, he does not dismiss it altogether. Even more significantly, he has discovered that there has been only one real attempt to test the hypothesis scientifically.

Writing of masturbation in their *Adolescent Development and Adjustment* (McGraw-Hill Book Company, 1965), Lester C. and Alice Crow conclude: "The effects of this form of sex perversion are not yet fully known."

Dr. David Horrobin, an M.D. and Ph.D. from Oxford University, states:

"The amount of zinc in semen is such that one ejaculation may get rid of all the zinc that can be absorbed from the intestines in one day. This has a number of consequences. Unless the amount lost is replaced by an increased dietary intake, repeated ejaculation may lead to a real zinc deficiency with various problems developing, including impotence.

"It is even possible, given the importance of zinc

for the brain, that 19th century moralists were correct when they said that repeated masturbation could make one mad!"—*Zinc* (Vitabooks: St. Albans, Vermont, 1981), p. 8.

This statement is similar to that made by Carl C. Pfeiffer, Ph.D., M.D., in his book on zinc. He declares:

"We hate to say it, but in a zinc-deficient adolescent, sexual excitement and excessive masturbation might precipitate insanity."—*Zinc and Other Micro-Nutrients* (Keats: New Canaan, Conn., 1978), p. 45.

Not all medical authorities would agree with these conclusions, yet it is significant that there are some whose study and research have led them to opinions which are compatible with the teachings of Ellen White.

See *Child Guidance*, pp. 439-456, for further information on this subject.

Appendix B

AN EARLY CHURCH PROBLEM

The first Seventh-day Adventist delegated State conference session, held at Monterey, Michigan, October 4-6, 1862, had before it four questions, the first of which was: "How shall we treat divorced marriages?"

The term "divorced marriages" was defined as marriages of spouses "who have been divorced from their former husbands or wives for other causes than that mentioned in Matthew 19, and under that divorce have married again. Shall such persons subsequently embracing present truth be received among us?" (RH Oct. 14, 1862.)

The matter was referred to the Conference Committee. No record can be found of any subsequent recommendation or action.